THE ESSENTIAL
QUILTER

TRADITION, TECHNIQUES, DESIGN, PATTERNS AND PROJECTS

BARBARA CHAINEY

THE ESSENTIAL
QUILTER

TRADITION, TECHNIQUES, DESIGN, PATTERNS AND PROJECTS

BARBARA CHAINEY

Photography by Roger Brown

Illustrations by Ken Goodwin

David & Charles

This book is dedicated to my father James Dyne Chainey
and also to three very special friends who did not live to
see its publication:
Sue Boulton, John Shone and Sally Gregory.

A DAVID & CHARLES BOOK

Text and illustrations Copyright © Barbara Chainey 1993
Photographs Copyright © Roger Brown 1993
First published 1993, reprinted 1994
First published in paperback 1997
Reprinted 1998

A catalogue record for this book is available from the
British Library.

ISBN 0 7153 0569 7

Typeset by Ace Filmsetting Ltd, Frome, Somerset
and printed in Italy by LEGO SpA
for David & Charles
Brunel House   Newton Abbot   Devon

CONTENTS

INTRODUCTION

'The quilting tradition is a skill from the living past which remains alive, enabling the quilter of today to create new beauty. It is in her hands, and in the hands of all who teach quilting to see that it is passed on alive to the future.'
Mavis Fitzrandolph, *Traditional Quilting* (1954)

I taught myself to quilt, picking my way through the few books then available and I can clearly recall my frustration and despair when reading that beginning quilters should make a seemingly impossible number of stitches per inch. As a consequence I developed what are politely called 'strong views'. First, quilt. Then try to quilt well. Do not worry about how your quilting is achieved. Enjoy the process for its own sake. Good quilting is not about size of stitch – even stitches are more important. Quilting should be as enjoyable to do as the resulting texture is pleasing to look at.

As a beginning quilter I found my practical progress slower than my appreciation of old quilts. Although I was entranced with colour and shape, it was always the quilting itself which captivated me and it remains a constant delight to see how the simplest materials and stitches combine to transcend the sum of their parts.

In general use, the term quilter refers to someone involved with any of the processes of making quilts. Similarly, quilting describes the activities involved in quiltmaking. For our purposes, a quilter is someone who stitches functional, decorative texture and quilting refers to the stitching itself.

WHAT IS A QUILT?

Any quilt is infinitely more than the sum of its parts. The top and back may be fashioned from patchwork, appliqué or plain (whole) cloth, padded with a layer of carded wool, cotton or synthetic wadding (batting), old blankets or even worn-out clothing. The three layers of the quilt are usually held together by stitching or tying. Quilts may be used for practical warmth or for decoration, and can be any size or shape from miniature to king-size.

DIFFERENT TYPES OF QUILT

Wholecloth quilts appear to be made from a single piece of cloth. This type of quilt is made from lengths of one cloth, plain or patterned, which are joined together to the required size. All the pattern on a wholecloth quilt is provided by the stitched texture.

Pieced quilts are exactly that – the top layer of the quilt, and sometimes the backing, are made up of small pieces or patches of different fabrics organised in a formal way and stitched together. The pieces may be made up into pattern units known as blocks which are then arranged or set in various ways, or the pieces may be joined together in an overall design.

Appliqué quilts differ from pieced quilts only in the technique used. Either fabric shapes are stitched or applied to a background and the patterns organised into blocks which are then set together, or the design may cover the whole quilt.

Strippy quilts represent the halfway mark between wholecloth and pieced quilts. Strips of fabric are joined in alternating sequence of contrast – hence the striped or stripped appearance which gives this type of quilt its name. The quilting designs are usually confined to the width of the strips, but may disregard the linear structure altogether.

Medallion is a term which refers to the arrangement of pieced, appliqué and wholecloth quilts where there is a well-defined centre surrounded by one or more borders.

HOW TO USE THIS BOOK

Chapter One looks briefly at the history of quilting and some of its distinctive traditions. If you are new to quilting, Chapters Two and Three describe preparation, quilting and finishing in detail. More experienced quilters may prefer to dip into Chapters Six and Eight for design sources and development. Chapter Four has some pointers for enhancing patchwork and appliqué with quilting. While the emphasis in this book is on hand quilting, the basics of machine quilting are outlined in Chapter Five, together with other forms of quilting. Chapter Seven shows traditional cable and feather patterns. Design principles and suggestions for adding that extra touch of originality are in Chapter Eight. Chapter Nine is for everyone who has a quilt, new or old. Project work is included throughout to encourage you to practise what I've preached!

Chapter One

HISTORY AND TRADITION

Quilting is an ancient and venerable craft and one that has been the subject of many changes of use over the centuries. It exists in many forms worldwide, and has undergone many alterations over the centuries, rising and falling in popularity and practice.

This ability to change and adapt is the hallmark of a successful craft, and during its long history quilting has shown itself to be admirably versatile. We assume that quilting originally developed from a need for warm clothing and bedding, but it is just as likely that quilting for warmth came after the craft was established as a decorative form of needlework.

Quilted fabrics have been used for protective armour, warm clothing, warm bedding and pure decoration. There are fine examples in museums around the world of early quilts dating from times when quilts were as much adornment for beds as providers of warmth. Everyday quilts from all periods have generally gone the way of the mundane and ordinary – used, worn out and often recycled beyond recognition.

THE PAST

THE 1700s

By the early 1700s quilting featured widely in costume – caps, petticoats, dresses and waistcoats – as well as bed ornamentation. However, it seems likely that quilts and quilted clothing remained the fashionable prerogative of the well-to-do. In the 1760s there was a rapid expansion in the UK of textile production, so cotton goods became more readily available and affordable. Imported cloth such as Indian painted cottons were very popular but too expensive to waste, giving rise to appliqué work to make the most of the intricate handpainted designs. More cloth = more clothes = more offcuts = patchwork. From this period patchwork developed alongside quilting.

THE 1800s

Quilts from the early 1800s are well represented in both museum and private collections. Often they have an elaborately and carefully pieced or appliqué top, with the quilting itself taking second place. Such quilts provide valuable evidence of types of fabrics and patterns, and of the printing and weaving techniques used at a time from which few clothes survive.

By the nineteenth century quilting was widely practised by that unsung background figure of all history – the ordinary woman. In North America quilting developed rapidly alongside patchwork as an essential thrift craft among the earliest settlers and by the early 1800s both were firmly part of the domestic and social round. The great push west on pioneer trails kept patchwork and quilting alive as necessary domestic crafts. Quilts were put to all manner of uses – tents; bedcovers and mattresses; doors, windows and even flooring; protection for precious crops and so on. Quilting as a social activity was one of the few opportunities many women had to enjoy a productive break from their considerable chores. Much has been recorded of quilting 'bees' where women worked together, but it would be wrong to think that this was the only way in which quilts were made. The majority of quilts on both sides of the Atlantic were the work of one woman and her close family – indeed, many skilled quilters preferred their work to be a solo effort with a consistent quality of stitching.

After 1875 a new bedcovering – the Marcella or Marseilles quilt – posed a considerable threat to the widespread popularity of the handmade quilt. These textiles were conceived as quilt lookalikes and were mass-produced following refinement of the new Jacquard loom. In a perverse twist of fashion, it became more desirable to own a Marcella spread than to have a handmade quilt, and for a short time many real quilts were used with the plain reverse side showing.

The latter half of the nineteenth century saw the finest flowering of both the patchwork and quilting traditions in the Old and the New Worlds. Patchwork had developed into a craft that was practical, economical and thrifty and it could be as simple or ornate as time and ability permitted. Quilting, while often linked with patchwork, continued to develop as a craft in its own right and many fine wholecloth quilts were produced from 1850 to 1900.

White and cream quilts from the North East of England

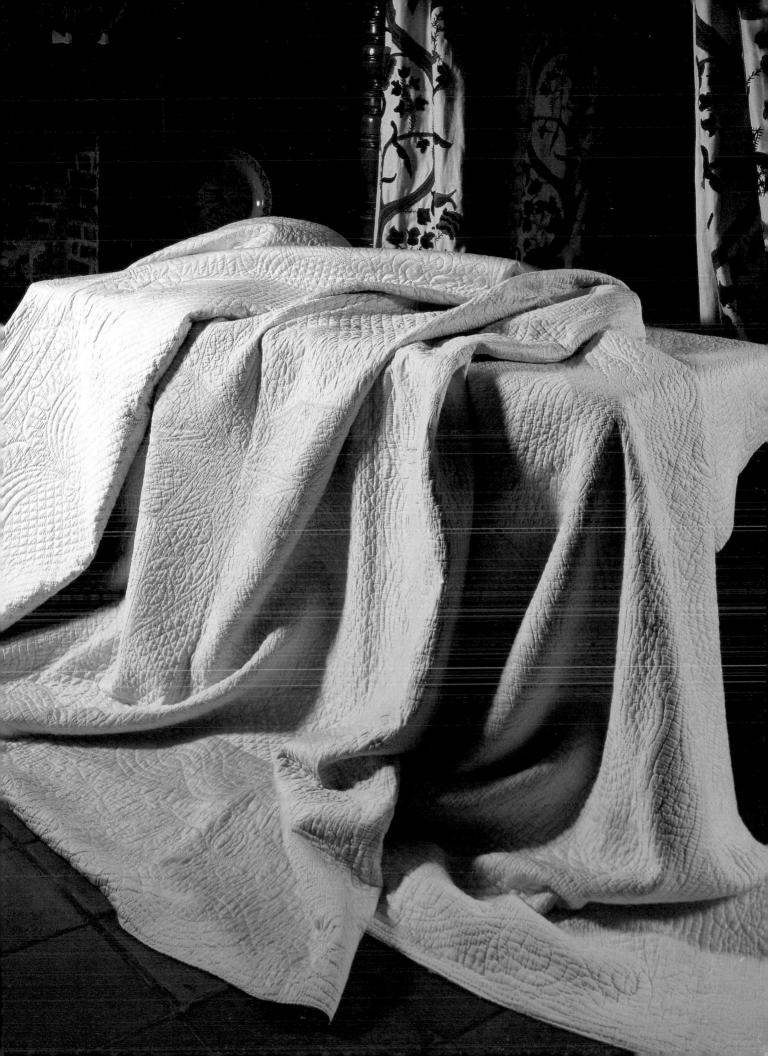

THE 1900s

World War I represents a watershed in the popularity of quilting. More and more manufactured goods of improved quality were available. It became fashionable to cover beds with eiderdowns, not quilts. Also growing numbers of women, traditionally the makers of quilts, had begun to move into the workplace. There was less time to quilt and less need. Quilts were nonetheless still made and used, particularly in rural areas which were less vulnerable to the whims of fashion. The quilt shown on page 123 was professionally designed in the Allenheads area of the North East of England in 1926 and lovingly stitched as a favourite daughter's bridal quilt. The daughter's reaction to the gift was expressive of the prevailing attitude – the quilt was dismissed as too 'old fashioned' and put away unused. Times of hardship and social change in the 1930s took their toll on quilting, although both patchwork and appliqué enjoyed a short-lived revival in the United States during the Depression years. In Britain by the early 1940s quilting was seen as a vanishing tradition worthy of recording and revival. The Rural Industries Bureau improved standards by organising commissioned work from some of the remaining quilters and by encouraging the teaching of traditional quilting skills.

The post-war years brought considerable changes to everyday life: increases in mobility, earning power, material acquisitions and mechanisation, and the stirrings of a consumer society geared to rapid changes in fashion. Those who quilted were few in number and the craft was viewed as old-fashioned and outdated. Quilting hovered on the brink of extinction until the early 1970s, when a phenomenal surge of interest in quilts as both domestic textiles and art forms originated just ahead of the American Bicentennial celebrations. This heralded a widespread international revival and relearning of the craft. Fortunately, there remained a small number of dedicated quilters, most taught literally at their mother's knees; their generous contribution of experience and sharing of their skills should not be underestimated.

While many wonderful quilts were made in the past (some quite breathtaking in technique and design), infinitely more were made with no aspirations to beauty or excellence, but in response to a need for warm bedding. Quilting may have been widely practised, but it was not always well done. Quilts in museum collections are most likely representations of the maker's best work, which received scant everyday use.

Quilting today is alive and well in many locations worldwide and people are discovering its satisfying and therapeutic benefits. Throughout Europe, North America, Japan and Australasia, there are flourishing quilt guilds, clubs, magazines and many exhibitions large and small, all providing a vital network of contacts, information and resources for quilters. Heritage programmes, aimed at adding to our fund of knowledge of quilts and their makers, are being undertaken with noteworthy results.

QUILTING TRADITIONS

In terms of style and use of patterns, there are three distinctive major traditions of quilting (as opposed to quilts), though many more exist. By looking at the salient features of these three, some idea of the framework on which present-day quilters may expand can be gleaned.

NORTH EAST ENGLAND

Quilting played an important part in domestic life in many North East villages before World War II – the meagre income that could be earned by quilting for others was a welcome addition to many households where the main breadwinner was invalided and unable to work or where widows were left to rear a family alone. Quilt clubs were organised whose members paid a fixed amount each week to the quilter, who made a quilt for each member in turn.

Many experienced quilters lacked the confidence to design quilts for themselves (does this sound familiar?) and so there was a demand for professionally marked quilt tops. The custom of sending tops to a professional marker was well-established in the North East from the time of Joseph Hedley 'Old Joe the Quilter'. Old Joe's fame and reputation as both quilter and marker of quilts was almost eclipsed by the violent manner in which he met his death in 1825, murdered (it is said) for the money he had supposedly amassed from quilting. George Gardiner was another, almost mythical, marker and designer, of whom little is known except that he kept a village shop in the latter half of the nineteenth century and was also noted as a hat-trimmer. One of his apprentices, Elizabeth Sanderson, built on what he had taught to become even better known in her own right.

The influence of both Gardiner and Sanderson on the surviving North East tradition is immense. Elizabeth Sanderson trained many apprentices who were able to pass her ideas and skills on to another generation after her death in 1934. The Gardiner style of design seemed to satisfy both local quilters and those from further afield; very little of the basic structure was subsequently altered, although the component patterns may have changed.

Quilts from the North East of England often have

Welsh quilts often combined strong colours with geometric shapes. (Quilts courtesy of Jen Jones)

A selection of traditional quilts made in the North East of England

formal but flowing patterns, carefully structured and arranged in either medallion or strippy style. There is a marked fondness for feather patterns, and background quilting contrasts well with the main pattern shapes. Many of the simple but rich crosshatching or diamond patterns on North East quilts are also found on Amish work.

Both the strippy and the wholecloth medallion style of quilt were, and still are, particularly popular and typify much of the regional tradition. The 'Gardiner/Sanderson' genre of wholecloth design – an ornate central design with deep borders, graceful corners and plentiful background quilting – is still favoured by today's quilters. This style is also widely found in old wholecloth quilts from both Europe and North America. Many quilts made in the North East had cotton wadding (batting), the standard of stitching was generally fine and a distinctive fabric, Roman Sateen, sadly no longer available, was popular for its attractive sheen and hard-wearing properties.

WALES

Quilts and quilting were as much part of the domestic round in Wales as in the North East, particularly in more remote villages. While the North East tradition produced professional quilt markers or stampers, the Welsh had itinerant quilters who travelled from farm to farm to ply their trade. The styles which typify the Welsh quilting tradition are wholecloth medallion, strippy and patchwork medallion, although these are by no means the only kinds of quilt produced. The piecing of many Welsh quilts is similar to that found in the Amish tradition, with clean strong lines and bold colour choices. Quilting patterns are frequently superimposed onto the pieced work rather than the design following the lines of the pieced shapes. The patterns themselves may be leaf, heart, tulip and spiral shapes (among others) arranged in an orderly manner, frequently around a central medallion. A somewhat limited range of patterns was used, but they have been freely adapted, scaled and interpreted. There may be one or more borders – quite often there are three – and the border patterns may stop at, rather than turn around, the quilt corners. The lines of quilting may be widely spaced compared to quilts from the North East, but there is much use of a double line to separate the main design areas and borders. The use of wool wadding, combined with sturdy fabrics for the top and backing, resulted in striking quilts which have a strongly sculptured quality.

Welsh quilters seem to have preferred carded wool wadding rather than cotton, although it is likely that, in rural areas that depended on sheep farming, wool was cheaper and easier to obtain than the prepared cotton favoured in the North East. Blankets, old clothes and rags were also used when necessary, and many a quilt was recycled by the simple expedient of re-covering it.

Despite working with unprepossessing ingredients, the Welsh quilters had an undeniable genius for bringing beauty out of simplicity. The quilting pattern in Fig 1 fits into a right angled triangle and is just one spiral (also called snail creep) and two short curved lines – nothing could be simpler. See what happens (Figs 1a and b) when several of these units are set together – a new pattern

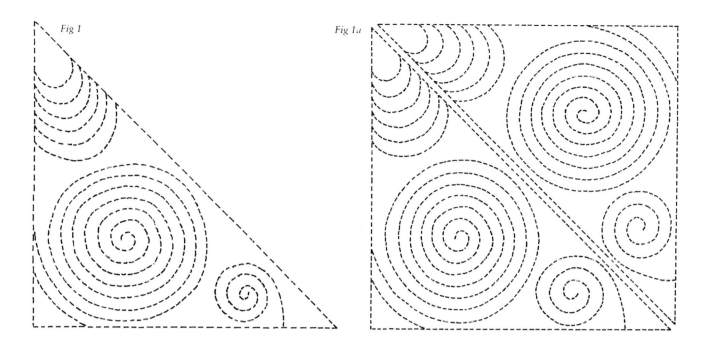

Fig 1

Fig 1a

Fig 1b

Two re-covered Welsh quilts. The one on the right has been restored sensitively and well; on the left is a hasty restoration complete with erratic machine quilting

emerges which, like a quilt, is greater than the sum of its parts.

Re-covering worn quilts and/or using old quilts as wadding was an economy measure done with varying degrees of care. The quilt above on the left shows the very crude and unimaginative re-covering of a once-lovely small Welsh quilt; two new fabrics have been stitched together by machine through all the layers. More sensitivity and care was shown by the unknown quilter who re-covered the other quilt with an early roller-printed fabric. Examining the inner fabrics – through a small tear in the top fabric and the worn edges of the newer quilt – show that the original quilt was pieced from sprigged muslins typical of the 1840s, some of which probably wore out quickly. But the re-covering has been done with

great care and skill, even to quilting a complete design through all five layers, which cannot have been easy.

Around the turn of the century there was a curious fashion for using patterned fabric on the quilt top. This could have been an attempt to update the appearance of quilts in line with the vogue for print-covered eiderdowns (which were expensive). This particular fashion could have contributed to the decline and deterioration in quilting standards because the textured pattern was almost completely obscured by the print.

NORTH AMERICA — THE AMISH

So many fine quilts were made throughout North America that it is almost impossible to select one single group for discussion. However, one particular quilting tradition, that of the Amish community, which is both highly

A pieced medallion Amish quilt shows fine quilting and rich glowing wool fabrics. A detail is shown on page 2. (Quilt courtesy of Bryce and Donna Hamilton)

distinctive and almost instantly recognisable, has had a considerable influence on many quilters. While there is no proven Amish quilting tradition before the mid-1800s, the quilts produced by this isolated and self-contained Christian sect were among the first to be viewed as textile art rather than purely practical bedcoverings.

The Amish culture embodies strong concepts of family and community; their world is that of a bygone era, where the technology of the twentieth century has no place and with great value placed on handwork and manual labour. Within this strictly regulated lifestyle, quilts were very much functional items but they also provided their makers with an expressive outlet. The workmanship on old Amish quilts is generally of the highest order, with simple piecing and strong, sombre colours used in what we might regard as an unconventional way. The main styles are the wholecloth medallion, strippy, pieced medallion and pieced block, and the quilting designs are almost without exception delicate in form and fine in execution. Characteristic quilting patterns include the fiddlehead fern (Fig 2), crosshatching, fan, roses, pumpkin seed, cables and feathered wreaths. Ornate quilting

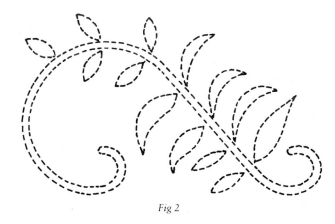

Fig 2

patterns are used to fill large spaces, almost always with a wonderful spare richness.

Unlike many of their British and American counterparts, Amish quilts were frequently dated and initialled in the quilting, which was often very fine and closely worked in black or dark thread. A padding of thin cotton or wool was customarily used, with wool or cotton fabric for both top and backing.

Old Amish quilts (pre-1940) seem to show common features which balance and contrast the piecing and the quilting stitches. There is an innate sense of what is 'enough' quilting and an ability to maintain an overall simplicity, such as a wonderful use of straight lines quilted over pieced blocks and strips to add texture without distracting from the lines of the pieced pattern.

THE FUTURE

There is much in each of these three traditions which is worthy of emulation; Welsh openness, vitality and simplicity, the North East organisation of simple patterns into great complexity; the ornate and precise Amish stitching enriching plain and often sombre fabric. In each, a willingness to adapt allowed the separate traditions to be maintained and to grow.

In Europe there was less input from a diminishing number of quilters, and it is possible that those who continued the tradition designed and stitched familiar styles and patterns. The variety of cultural input from European immigrants in North America benefitted quilting and both pieced work and quilting flourished. This vigour and these strong traditions had a powerful influence in the early 1970s when the renewal of interest in American quilting heritage triggered a similar revival in Europe.

Quilting today is in a very healthy and transitional state – it is increasingly popular as a craft and rapidly developing within and beyond the broad framework of what has gone before. New materials, especially wadding (batting), allow a greater freedom of expression in spacing the pattern since close quilting is no longer needed to hold it in place. A brief vogue for minimal quilting seems to have been superseded by a return to close quilting on both wholecloth and pieced and appliqué quilts, many of which have no practical need of the considerable amount of quilting worked on them. Experimentation with machine quilting offers many exciting new possibilities and promises much for the future. Many quilters are taking up the challenge of re-working and adapting existing traditional pieces, and traditional patterns are being used in new arrangements.

Art quilts are a major and exciting development from within the mainstream of quilting. They and their makers challenge much that is considered traditional and 'correct' and expand the entire range of quilting. Committed traditionalists can learn much from this eclectic experimentation with quilted texture. Because they are made to hang rather than to spread, these quilts force the viewer to consider colour, shape and texture in abstract ways, for their own sake rather than as incidental.

Quilting is no longer practised to satisfy economic or social needs, but for expression and enjoyment. In this age of fast communications and travel, a wide range of ideas and influences is exchanged quickly and easily. Specific traditions have inevitably been diluted but this is still a most exciting time to be involved in the ongoing development of quilting.

Chapter Two

EQUIPMENT, FABRICS AND MARKING

he basic equipment for quilting begins with fabric, wadding (batting) and backing and continues with needles, pins, thread, scissors, thimble, beeswax and preferably some sort of frame or hoop to quilt on. A long ruler, masking tape, drawing paper and a marker for transferring patterns onto fabric are other necessities.

FABRICS FOR QUILTING

TOP OF THE QUILT

The choice and preparation of fabrics is as important in quilting as it is for patchwork. The relief of quilting shows to good advantage on fabrics with a glazed or satinised finish – silks, satins, polished cottons, etc. Quilting can also transform humble cottons to the heights of sophistication. Plain-weave fabric, in which threads cross each other at right angles, is often best as stitches that fall between the threads of a twill weave where threads cross diagonally, can lose a considerable amount of impact.

If possible, avoid tightly woven fabrics such as percale, sheeting and some polycottons which have a high thread count/number of threads to the inch. These are so difficult to quilt through that progress can be slow and frustrating. Polycotton fabrics do not generally respond well to quilting and the results are frequently very disappointing. If you use 100% cotton fabric, wash it first so that any

Equipment needed for hand quilting

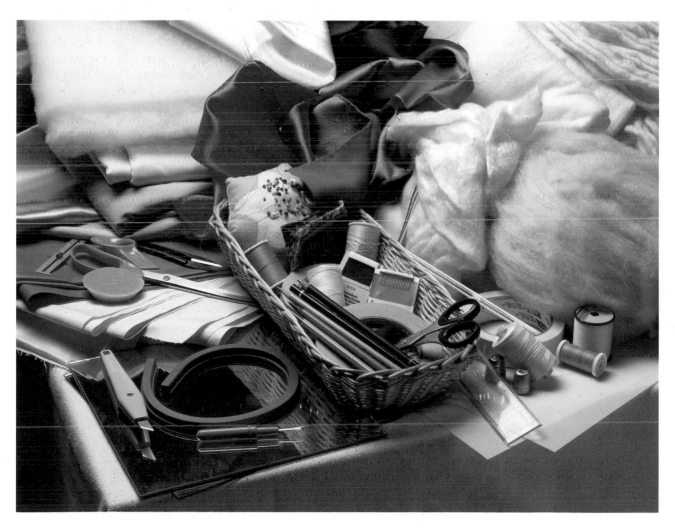

shrinkage occurs before you begin quilting. If you want a traditional look, try washing after the quilting is complete, especially if you plan to use a cotton wadding (batting) – any shrinkage will then add to the traditional effect.

Average-quality quilting always looks good on high-quality fabrics – treat yourself to the best you can afford. Furnishing-weight fabrics present difficulties; they are dense and heavy and will not show much 'loft', the height or depth of the quilted pattern. Glazes on furnishing fabrics are often thick and sometimes brittle. The glaze may diminish or disappear with laundering, showing every needle hole clearly and allowing the wadding to filter through. Loosely woven fabrics may also allow wadding to escape, or 'beard'.

JOINING FABRIC FOR TOP

It is usually best to join fabrics for a wholecloth quilt by using one full width of fabric for the centre panel, flanked by partial or full widths on each side so that the seams run from top to bottom of the completed top (Fig 3a). Avoid a central seam running either from side to side or top to bottom since a centre seam is always more noticeable.

BACKING FABRIC

The considerations for choosing fabric for the backing or third layer of a quilt will be the same as those for the quilt top. A strong pattern or colour used on the reverse may 'shadow' through and be visible from the front of a light-coloured quilt. A subdued print or a pale plain (solid) fabric would be a better choice for backing a patchwork or appliqué quilt top as well. Prints are nevertheless a popular choice for backing patchwork quilts, because quilting stitches show less on print fabrics, which can be kinder to first attempts at quilting.

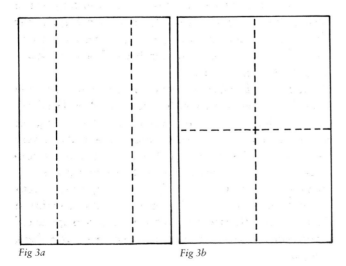

Fig 3a   *Fig 3b*

PREPARING BACKING FABRIC

You may find it necessary to join the backing fabric so that it is wide or long enough. A centre seam running either horizontally or vertically is one choice (Fig 3b), or you could use one full width of fabric with half a width on each side, as shown in Fig 3a.

Avoid having unnecessary seams on the backing; they will only make extra thicknesses to quilt through. Remember to trim off any selvages before seaming the fabric together; they are very closely woven and quilting through them is difficult.

For the backing fabric, it is usual to match the composition and weight of the top fabric(s). If your top is 100% dressweight cotton, that would be best for the backing. A few of my students have experimented with sheeting – both polycotton and cotton – and have regretted their choice. Sheeting generally is too densely woven to be pierced easily with a needle and this outweighs any advantage of price and width.

WADDING (BATTING)

Today's quilter has a wide choice of wadding – the traditional cotton, wool and blanket waddings are still available. Synthetic polyester wadding, today's most popular choice, can be bought pre-cut in standard sizes and also off the bolt in a variety of weights and thicknesses, with 2-ounce and 4-ounce weights the most usual. It can be very difficult to quilt through 4-ounce wadding, which is best reserved for machine-quilting or items where warmth and high loft are important. The market compromise exists as a mixed cotton and synthetic wadding, usually sold in pre-cut sizes. Both this and pure cotton wadding respond well to gentle rinsing and drying before use, which softens the fibres slightly and makes quilting easier.

Most waddings by law have a special fire-retardant coating which may make needling less easy – rinsing and drying before use should make it more pliable.

Dense 'needlepunched' waddings are an ideal choice for machine quilting if a firm, low loft is required. If you will be working with predominantly dark fabrics, dark grey waddings are available that cut down on visible bearding.

PREPARING WADDING

Most synthetic wadding is sold in a variety of widths and weights. It can easily be butted together and joined with a ladder or lacing stitch if necessary (Fig 4).

You may, with care, be able to split or peel wadding apart if a particularly thin layer is required.

Silk wadding is becoming increasingly popular, both

Fig 4

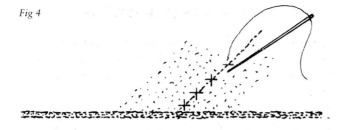

for decorative quilted clothing and larger quilts. Silk wadding can be bought loose or from the bolt in varying thicknesses. Its lightness and warmth make it particularly suitable for clothing, and it is very easy to quilt through.

Loose silk wadding, like carded wool, can be laid in position on the backing without joining. Silk off the roll can be joined like synthetic wadding Fig. 4. Quilted items with silk wadding should be laundered in cool water and gentle soap and with minimum agitation.

Wool wadding can now be obtained by the yard. Like silk, it offers a high degree of warmth, but is fractionally heavier and even easier to quilt through. A well-prepared wool wadding has a lot to recommend it and deserves wider use.

Many traditional quilters layered fine muslin or cheese-cloth over the carded wool between the top and backing of the quilt to prevent bearding. Clean hand-carded wool is easiest to use when working on a traditional frame. Set out one frameful on the backing, lay the top over and quilt, repeating the process as the quilt requires rolling on. If you would like to use wool wadding, but are unable to obtain it ready-prepared, a local group of spinners, weavers and dyers may be able to help. Soaking in cool water with a little soap, minimum agitation followed by a short spin and a rinse are all that is usually necessary for the laundering and aftercare of wool wadding.

Cotton wadding is usually sold in ready-cut standard bed sizes. All-cotton wadding is slightly difficult to quilt; it resists the needle and requires close quilting to prevent it from becoming lumpy when washed. If you want to try all-cotton wadding, lay out the wadding in a warm place to allow it to expand slightly before use. This expansion may make quilting a little easier.

Flannel, domette and blanket are all woven fabrics that can be used as wadding for a quilt. They are more difficult to quilt than, say, synthetic wadding if you plan to quilt by hand, but are well suited to machine-quilting where a low loft is required.

Whatever type of wadding you choose, buy the best quality you can. Prepared waddings are often superior to cheaper waddings sold off the roll.

Bearding is the term used to describe the visible migration of wadding fibres through the fabric, resulting in unsightly fuzz on the surface of the quilt.

THREADS

Today's quilter can choose from a wide variety of threads, from quilting thread to ordinary sewing thread to specialist embroidery threads. Quilting thread can be 100% cotton or cotton-covered polyester, both available in a good choice of colours. Some quilting threads are, however, difficult to thread through the eye of finer betweens needles.

THICKNESS OF THREAD

Lovers of fine hand quilting may hesitate to use traditional quilting thread, feeling that it is too thick for closely quilted projects which will receive minimal wear and tear. Standard cotton sewing thread as fine as 50s-count is satisfactory and offers a wide choice of colours and shades. New quilting threads continue to come onto the market and are worth trying – everyone has a particular favourite.

TYPE OF THREAD

It is obviously sensible to match thread to fabric type – for example, using silk thread with silk fabric and wadding. Polyester threads are widely used in home sewing and may be used when quilting with polyester satins. However this thread has a tendency to fray at the eye of the needle and, unlike cotton thread, it stretches. Use shorter lengths of thread and a finer needle than usual.

COLOUR OF THREAD

Unless you are working with black or white fabric, the effect will be better if the colour of fabric and thread do not match exactly. Thread that is one or two shades darker than the fabric will enhance the texture the quilting creates. Thread which matches the fabric exactly or is a shade lighter can give a spotty effect which spoils the impact of the quilted lines. Quilting creates a furrow or depression in the fabric and your thread should match this slightly darker shading.

Contrasting thread If you examine some old quilts, you may find that an outrageously contrasting thread has been used which reveals itself only at close quarters. A brighter or much darker contrasting thread can make a very positive contribution to your design; for example, a deep pink or blue thread on pale pink or blue fabric gives subtle shading and emphasis. Highly contrasting thread looks good if you have average-length stitches. A coarse thread can also be effective but take care and perhaps avoid contrasting or coarse threads for your first few quilting projects.

FANCY THREADS AND SPECIAL EFFECTS

There is now a wonderful selection of metallic, variegated and shaded sewing threads available, many of which are suitable for quilting. Some fray easily and need careful handling, but the results can be stunning. For instance, a shaded blue metallic thread worked as random lines would suggest the flow, movement and reflections of water.

FRAMES

Gone are the days when the quilting frame was an integral part of many households. The development of a portable quilting frame in the form of a hoop or hoop on a stand was a major breakthrough which made the craft more accessible. The ultra-portable tubular clip frame is an equally important innovation. The main advantage of this particular type of frame is that it holds the textile sandwich foursquare over a rounded profile. Compare this with compressing a quilt over the thin inner ring of a hoop, with some portions of the 'sandwich' being stretched on full bias.

Anyone who has sufficient space to set up a traditional fixed frame is fortunate. Traditional frames can be as basic or sophisticated as you like and can afford. Whether you use four lengths of wood with clamps or a free-standing frame, the main difference between the traditional static and the modern portable frame is that with a static frame you will have to go to your quilt; a portable frame can go with you. Portable frames can be turned and manoeuvred as you work so that you are always stitching in the easiest direction. Traditional frames cannot be turned – you and your hands make all the adjustments – and they require different setting up and preparation; the portable frame requires thorough tacking (basting) of the layers before quilting can begin.

Many quilters eschew the use of a frame altogether, and quilt a firmly tacked sandwich in their laps with more than acceptable results. Except for very small projects [less than 10 inches (25 cm) square], lap quilting does not work well for everyone. Pleats, tucks and puckers can occur easily and remain undetected until it is too late to correct them.

WHICH FRAME?

Many beginning quilters are unsure about using a frame and wonder which is the best type to choose. Of course, three layers can be quilted without a frame, but a better result is usually obtained with a frame of some sort. A frame holds the quilt layers square under some tension, which leaves your hands free to concentrate on quilting.

Frames available for quilting include the traditional fixed wooden frame, large hoops and tubular clip frames in large and small sizes

Quilting worked on a frame often has a crisper loft and fewer puckers than quilting worked without a frame. The thought of using a frame can be a little worrying – it can make everything seem too technical and far-removed from sewing for pleasure. Just tell yourself that this is a professional way of going about things and try. Some quilters mix and match frames, using a traditional frame to work basic outline quilting and then transferring the work to a portable frame to stitch more intricate patterns.

SETTING UP A TRADITIONAL FRAME

Frames come in many styles and sizes, and there is one that will suit you and the way you want to work. The simplest is the large static frame made from four lengths of timber and virtually identical to an embroiderer's slate frame. Two lengths of wood have webbing or other strong fabric attached to them – these rails are usually the width of the work or more in length. Two shorter pieces of wood – the stretchers – brace the rails and are held in position with clamps or pegs, and may also have holes drilled to allow adjustment of the working depth of the frame. All three layers – top, wadding and backing – are attached to the webbing of the near rail with neat tacking (basting) stitches. The backing is then tacked to the webbing on the opposite rail and wound on until it is stretched evenly between the two rails. The position is maintained by completing the frame with the stretchers.

The wadding and top fabric are then carefully laid over the taut backing and pinned through all three layers as shown in Fig 5, page 22. Surplus wadding and top fabric hang over the far rail until the exposed area has been quilted and it is time to roll the work on. Lengths of tape are pinned into place on each side of the work to ensure even tension. Many variations of this type of frame are available. You can buy a frame with its own stand; rails

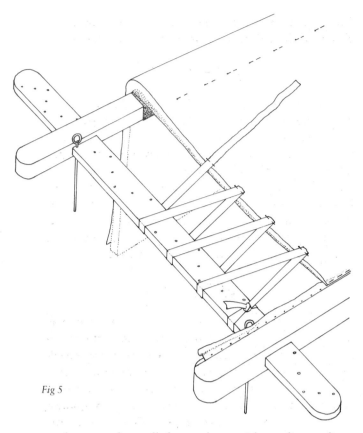

Fig 5

can be rotated to roll the work on without dismantling; the positions of rail and stretcher can be locked with ratchets, dispensing with the need for clamps or drilled holes; the whole working area of the frame can be tilted and locked at different angles. Further improvements exist in the form of a third rail which holds only the backing fabric and allows the wadding and top fabric to be wound around the second rail, and at least one frame can be folded flat against a wall without needing to remove the work. Instructions for making a frame can be purchased from suppliers who advertise in specialist quilting magazines.

One of the advantages of this type of frame is that no tacking (basting) of the quilt layers is required. This alone makes many quilters look favourably on traditional frames. Once the quilt is set up, it is always ready if there are a few spare moments for stitching. A quilt frame can also provide extra work space if it is covered with a sheet and then a lightweight board. The 'loft' of a quilt stitched on this type of frame is slightly higher and crisper than otherwise, because no pre-handling or tacking is required which flattens the layers.

If the sheer size of a traditional frame makes it unsuitable, a smaller version is available. This smaller size is useful if you wish to quilt a quilt one block at a time (usually referred to as 'quilt-as-you-go') and join the blocks or sections together after quilting, and for making smaller items such as crib quilts and cushions.

OTHER OPTIONS

Static traditional frames are generally between four feet and eight feet (1.25 m to 2.75 m) in length. Visitors, family and friends can be trained to negotiate an obstacle of this size, but several smaller options are available.

Hoops Perhaps you have seen other quilters using a hoop similar to an embroidery hoop. These are available in various sizes and can be mounted on a floor stand if required. The two rings of the hoop will accommodate the thickness of a quilt between them and can be adjusted by means of a screw.

Some hoops can be rotated while fixed to the stand – this ideal arrangement combines easy movement with maximum support.

All hoops offer a highly portable and lightweight frame on which to quilt and can be turned easily so that you are always working in a comfortable direction. If you try to quilt complex curving lines on a traditional frame, you will soon see why hoops are so popular! Quilting a large piece on a hoop also has tremendous draughtproofing qualities and by carefully arranging the folds the quilter can be kept extremely cosy. It has been suggested that a round hoop holds the work at a more even tension than its oval counterpart, but many quilters find the oval hoop less cumbersome.

The main disadvantage of using any sort of hoop is the amount of tacking (basting) required before beginning to quilt. Lack of tacking or insufficient tacking allows the three layers to shift as the hoop is moved from one part of the quilt to another. Everyone hates tacking, but it is absolutely essential if you plan to work on anything except a traditional frame. Why not turn it into a social occasion and invite several friends to share the chore? Tacking itself is discussed in somewhat more detail in Chapter Three.

Setting up a hoop Stretch the tacked quilt smoothly over the inner ring and push the outer ring down over it to hold the quilt in position; then tighten the screw to secure it. With a round or oval hoop, make sure the work is not unduly stretched, but smooth and wrinkle-free on both sides. The quilt is being gripped with considerable pressure and stretched over the high thin profile of the inner ring. Therefore do not leave your work in the hoop any longer than necessary – overnight is too long. Get into the Good Habit of removing your work from the hoop each time you finish a stint of quilting. Leaving the quilt in a hoop for any length of time may cause creases, folds and occasionally stains from unsealed wood. Some quilters like to bind both rings of the hoop with strips of fabric to increase the grip; this is not essential, but do check that the wood has been well sealed to prevent stains. The diameter of hoop is a matter of personal choice; one student with a very busy lifestyle was happier working with a small hoop which meant she could achieve a target of quilting one hoopful each evening.

TUBULAR FRAMES

Square tubular frames also require much the same preparation of quilt layers as hoops: thorough tacking worked systematically. This type of frame is very similar to a hoop, except that it is much simpler to adjust the tension of the layers by moving the holding clips, and keeping the layers smooth seems easier. Remove the holding clips each time you finish quilting or you may find permanent grooves in the fabric.

NEEDLES

If you already have an assortment of sewing needles, chances are that amongst them will be some betweens, very short stubby needles with a slightly rounded eye that range from coarse to fine – the higher the number, the finer the needle. The preferred size of needle varies from one quilter to another. Quilting through three layers where the wadding (batting) and fabrics are all light-weight is easy with 9 or 10 betweens but the same needle will not necessarily be suitable for dense wadding and heavy fabrics. Choose a needle size that you can thread fairly easily (make a note to have your eyesight checked soon) and is as fine as you can comfortably manage. If you are new to quilting, 8 or 9 betweens are a safe choice – the best results are most often obtained from using a short, fairly fine needle. Invest in a pack or two of assorted betweens and experiment. A Good Quilting Habit to acquire is always having several needles threaded, whether they are left on the spool of thread ready to be drawn off one at a time, or pushed into a pincushion near your work.

PINS

Any pins that you use should be fine, sharp, long and rustfree. Glass-headed pins have that little blob of colour to help you locate the pin when it drops onto your lap, the dog or the carpet. The best place to store pins is in a pincushion, tin or box, not stuck into your sweater, gripped between your teeth or resting in the furniture.

SCISSORS

Well-sharpened shears are for cutting lengths of fabric and wadding (batting) and should be kept strictly for that purpose. Never use the same scissors for cutting fabric and paper; you will only blunt them. A small pair of scissors or snips is all you need to clip quilting threads.

Snub-ended scissors and snips are better as there is less chance of the points accidentally nicking the fabric.

BEESWAX

Some quilters wax their thread so automatically that they do so irrespective of need. Many quilting threads are advertised as not requiring waxing before use. Again, it is a matter of personal choice. If you wax the thread, pull it lightly across the cake of wax once or twice and run the thread between finger and thumb to remove any excess. If you are using ordinary sewing thread, waxing can reduce, but not eliminate, the number of knots and tangles as you stitch. The fine wax coating also helps the thread to glide through the fabric layers more easily.

THIMBLES

There are various schools of thought and practice as to the use of thimbles when quilting. Some protection is necessary for the finger which will push the needle through the quilt layers. Even if you have never worn a thimble before, common sense will tell you to persevere. A great divergence of opinion appears among the quilting fraternity on the question of protection for the non-sewing or underneath hand. Some insist on the need to protect the fingers of the underneath hand from being pricked. Others cannot quilt unless they feel the point of the needle, thus reassuring themselves that it has gone through all three layers. If you are one of the latter, resign yourself to quilting for short periods only so that your fingers do not get too sore or bloody, and ultimately to developing callouses on your fingertips. Frequent applications of surgical spirit (rubbing alcohol) may help harden the skin. Blood stains and spots can be removed with saliva and/or cold water.

Otherwise you must decide how to protect your fingers. In addition to the usual metal or leather thimble, the choices range from the cut-off finger of a leather glove, surgical gloves, banker's rubber finger covers, surgical tape, plastic bandages, clear nail varnish – the choice is only limited by ingenuity. There is even a thimble designed to accommodate long fingernails! Even if you wear an ordinary metal thimble on your non-sewing hand, there is a choice. In his seminal book *The Quiltmaker's Handbook* (Prentice Hall, 1978) American quilter Michael James advocated the use of a thimble with a flat top which creates a slight ridge through the layers of the quilt. Almost overnight hundreds, perhaps thousands, of quilters flattened their thimbles and 'ridge top' thimbles soon appeared on the market. More recently, very smooth thimbles intended to help the needle glance or glide off their surface have been introduced and doubtless other aids will follow. If you use a metal thimble on your non-sewing hand, you may find that needles become blunt quite quickly, but this is perhaps a minor problem compared to sore fingers.

PREPARING TO QUILT
PREPARING THE QUILT TOP

Press the backing fabric thoroughly, paying particular attention to opening and flattening the seam allowances. For a patchwork top give special thought to the many seam allowances and the direction in which they need to be pressed, so there are a minimum of allowances to quilt through. Appliqué tops should be pressed from the wrong side of the work on a padded surface – put one or two clean old towels on the ironing board. (Pressing appliqué from the right side can make the slightly raised edges of the shapes unattractively shiny.) Take a last look at the wrong side and carefully clip or trim any loose threads.

MARKING METHODS

The aspect of quiltmaking that raises the most questions, controversy and wonderment is marking. Among the most frequently asked questions at any practical quilting demonstration are 'How has the pattern been put on to the fabric? Will the marking come off when it is finished? How will the marks be removed?' Marking skills depend largely on being aware of the methods and tools available. Quilters today have a wide choice, but there is no single perfect, easily removable, way of marking every available fabric. The ideal marker or method would make a fine line which would remain clearly visible while quilting was in progress and would then be easily removed. Ease and completeness of removal is probably more important than speed of removal. Since the choice of marking tools continues to grow, the following list cannot be comprehensive, but gives an idea of the various possibilities.

Marking a design is usually done before the three quilt layers are tacked (basted) together, so you can work with a single flat layer of fabric. To guarantee accuracy, keep the point or edge of any marking tool as close as possible to the actual line or edge of the pattern, stencil or template. Always test any marker or method for yourself.

Tailors' chalk Many beginning quilters assume that this useful piece of dressmaking equipment will also be suitable for quilting. It has been used in the past for lack of alternatives, but it generally smudges and rubs off too easily and produces too thick a line.

Ordinary pencil has its uses, but graphite can stay firmly embedded in the quilting thread and result in lines of grubby stitches. Heavy pencil lines can be almost impossible to remove. Water-soluble pencils are available from art shops. These are very soft and need only the lightest pressure to make a mark on fabric. The line made by hard-leaded pencils may be difficult to see. An HB or B pencil, well-sharpened and used lightly, may be better, but take care not to drag the fabric as you mark. Automatic or propelling pencils make a fine line and do not need constant sharpening. One such pencil is being marketed as easy to use and remove but still requires care with lightness of touch.

Chalk pencils are often pink with a small brush at one end for erasing the chalk. The line produced is quite broad and can, like tailor's chalk, brush off too quickly. This type of pencil requires a little pressure to make a mark and could be unsuitable for lightweight fabrics.

Powdered chalk Refillable pouches of white or coloured powdered chalk with a small slit and wheel at one end produce a crisp fine line with ease. Chalks offer only temporary marking, but this seems to last longer than most and is excellent for use with slotted stencils. An ideal way to mark dark fabrics a little at a time.

Water soluble pens These pens were once thought to be the answer to every quilter's prayer – they make a clear blue line which can be sponged or misted out with cold water. They produce a thick line and stitches can wander from one side to the other, with wobbly results. Do test on fabric before use. Heat, sunlight or even warm water can 'set' the line permanently into an unattractive brown colour, and damp or steamy conditions can remove it prematurely. Immerse the fabric in cold water to remove the marks before ironing or washing; these processes can set the colour. If you sponge or mist with cold water, blue tide marks may appear later.

Fade-out pens, heralded as an excellent marking tool at first, are now thought to cause premature weakening and rotting of fabrics – a factor to consider if you are embarking on an 'heirloom' quilt. (Aren't they all going to be heirlooms when first we begin?)

Water soluble crayons are inexpensive and widely available in a range of colours. Sponging will remove faint lines; gentle washing will be needed for more definite ones. They are not as easy to sharpen as a pencil, but do produce a fine line. There is a good choice of colours, so they can be used on fabric of virtually any colour. Some may be more difficult to remove than others – test first on a scrap of fabric.

Silver/soapstone pencils have become increasingly popular. They are easy to sharpen and visible on most fabrics. Washing usually removes marks completely.

Coloured pencils are sometimes more difficult to remove than water-soluble ones. Used lightly, crayon should wash out, but do test first. Professional quilt markers or stampers in the North of England often used

The prick and pounce method of marking a pattern using powdered cinnamon

Needlemarking around wooden templates

a blue or yellow crayon, perhaps in emulation of the renowned Elizabeth Sanderson's favoured marker. The social cachet of a professionally marked quilt meant that many were never laundered for fear of removing the crayon lines.

Chinagraph pencil is waxy and not easy to sharpen. One of Britain's best-loved traditional quilters, Mrs Amy Emms MBE, uses it with great success.

Dressmakers carbon is transferred to fabric by running a dried-up ballpoint pen or tracing wheel over the design with the carbon sheet between design and fabric. It can be difficult to remove; testing is strongly recommended. The heat of an iron or hot water can set the carbon indelibly – use with extreme caution.

Office carbon is suitable for paper, but almost impossible to remove from fabric. Generally classed as one of the Nevers of quilt marking.

Soap is a good water-soluble marker popular with traditional quilters. Slivers of air-hardened soap make useful markers for dark fabrics and give a reasonably fine line.

Prick and pounce, a well-established method for embroidery, can be useful for marking delicate and/or dark fabrics. Draw the design on tracing paper, set your unthreaded sewing machine to 4–6 stitches per inch, and, using an old needle, stitch through the paper along all the pattern lines. Alternatively, use a darning needle and the services of a willing ten-year-old to make the perforations

by hand, but remember this can be tedious if the pattern is large or complex.

Lay the completed perforated pattern on top of the fabric and tape both securely in position. Shake powder (talcum, chalk or cinnamon, depending on the colour of the fabric) over the paper and work it carefully through the perforations with a small pad of cotton wool (absorbent cotton). Remove the tape and lift the pattern sheet up in one smooth movement, taking care not to smudge the dots of powder. The dots can now be connected with another marker if necessary. This is not the fastest marking method, but useful for smaller projects.

Tacking (basting) involves stitching the design outlines on fabric through a tissue paper tracing which is then torn away leaving the tacked lines as a guide for quilting.

Tissue paper, a method suitable for delicate fabrics, involves marking or tracing the design on tissue paper which is then tacked onto the fabric. The quilting is worked through both the tissue paper and the quilt layers. The tissue paper can be torn away, a little at a time, as quilting progresses.

Needlemarking/'scratching', once far more popular and familiar than it is today, is worthy of making a comeback. There are no coloured markings to remove, and the marks are reasonably resilient to the minimal handling associated with working on a static frame, but less suitable when using a hoop or portable frame.

Needlemarking is usually executed with a rug or

Marking a quilt top using templates – feathers – and stencils – cables

Tracing a pattern through thin, pale-coloured fabric

darning needle set into a cork for easier handling – a cobbler's awl may also be suitable. Place a soft pad, such as a folded blanket, on your work surface and position the fabric on top. Hold the point at an oblique angle, close against the edge of a template, and press down onto the fabric to make a sharp crease which will be visible on pale and/or shiny fabrics such as some silks, satins, glazed and unglazed cottons. You can needlemark around a template, or through a stencil or tissue paper design. If you mark through tissue paper, make a duplicate of the design before you begin, otherwise you will only have shredded paper to return to your pattern file. (You do keep a pattern file, don't you?)

A relatively new tool for this type of marking is now available. Based on a traditional Japanese marking tool, it is easy to handle and gives a good sharp crease.

Stencils and templates can be made from plastic, card, metal or wood. An increasingly wide and attractive choice of commercial plastic stencils is available. They can be particularly useful for marking a little at a time on a traditional frame or hoop and for marking dark or difficult fabrics from the top.

If you feel hesitant about marking directly onto the quilt top with either templates or stencils, practise on paper first to build up your confidence.

If you are worried about fabric shifting as you mark,

slide a sheet of very fine grade sandpaper underneath to hold the fabric in position as you work.

A template is a shape to be marked around with inner lines marked freehand. A stencil has cut channels which allow both inner and outer lines to be marked. Templates and stencils can easily be made at home.

Templates can be made by tracing individual patterns and gluing them onto good-quality card or mounting board. The card can then be cut to shape with a sharp craft knife. Scissors will cut lighter-weight card. Acetate sheets, x-ray film or flattened plastic containers are all suitable for recycling as template material. Cereal box card is too flimsy for templates that will be used a lot. A commercial opaque or frosted plastic which cuts easily with scissors is ideal for template making. It gives a firm edge and does not wear down with repeated use.

Stencils can be made in much the same way as templates. Cut the channels carefully, these have to be wide enough for a pencil or marker point to move along freely. If you are using opaque plastic, use a craft knife to cut the channels rather than manoeuvre scissor blades in a very restricted area. A 'hot pen' simplifies channel cutting, or holes can be punched instead of channels.

Tracing If you use light-coloured fabric, draw the design on white paper with a black marker. Position the design on a firm smooth surface, with the fabric on top.

Tape both layers so that no movement is possible. Trace the lines onto the fabric with your preferred marker. A bright lamp moved nearer to the work may make it even easier to see the design.

Light boxes are useful if you are marking dark fabrics. The simplest form of light box is a sheet of glass or clear plastic with its edges taped for safety and balanced on books or blocks high enough to slide a table lamp underneath. Remember though, lamps get hot, and both fabric and paper are flammable. You can buy a portable light box or have one made.

A large sunny window makes a fine vertical light box for marking small projects – marking a large piece this way is fraught with problems and aching arms. For really small projects [less than 24 inches (60 cm) square] you could adapt the lightbox which resides in most homes – the television. Switch on the video channel, tape pattern and fabric to the screen and mark away. Avoid peak family viewing times when trying this method.

Self-adhesive plastic offers a temporary marking method with no telltale lines to remove afterwards, but pre-test on delicate fabrics for adhesive residue. Cut out your design shapes, remove the paper backing, position the shapes on your fabric and quilt around them. These films are re-usable several times before good adhesion is lost. The shapes give a good clear edge to quilt against but be wary of leaving them on the fabric for any length of time – sticky residue is difficult to remove and may discolour.

Masking tape is a wonderful way to help you quilt those crisp straight lines we all admire, without having to mark everything out first. Masking tape is cheap, readily available and comes in a variety of widths. A 'crepe' version, available from hardware shops, can be used for making curved guide lines. Quilting suppliers have a ¼ inch (0.6 cm) width tape which can go around curves if you clip one side as you place it on the fabric. Most tape can be used more than once before it is scrunched up into a ball to help remove fluff, cat hair and crumbs from your work.

Canvas is a sneaky way of marking lines onto fabric accurately and fairly easily. Lay wide-mesh rug canvas over the fabric and draw down the canvas with your preferred marker at regular intervals, say every fifth hole to leave a dotted line on the fabric.

Net Draw your design on fairly wide-mesh net with a waterproof pen (test the waterproof factor first). Then lay the net over the fabric and draw over the marked lines with your fabric marker. This will leave a dotted line for you to follow.

Photocopiers not only enlarge or reduce patterns in a matter of seconds, but a fresh (less than two hours old) photocopy can be used to transfer patterns onto light fabric. Put the photocopy face down on the right side of

Masking tape and self-adhesive film are useful for marking quilting patterns

the fabric and iron over it, using a warm/hot setting but no steam. Remove the paper carefully; your fabric is marked ready for use. Try this method out on a spare piece of fabric first and test for ease of removal.

Other aids One essential tool is a long ruler with clear markings. Many quilters' rulers have 90°, 45° and 60° angles marked and are a minimum of 18 inches (45 cm) long. Keen quilters will find many uses for a plexiglass rod known as a quilter's quarter and a flexicurve, which can be bent around simple shapes and curves to produce single lines, parallel lines and echo lines of consistent width. A hem gauge is handy for checking seam allowances and making sure the spacing between lines is consistent.

The most popular methods for marking out are tracing, light box, and stencils and templates. Lacking a single perfect marking tool, each quilter develops personal preferences. Whatever your choice of marker, it is up to you to check for ease of removal.

To remove marks, intentional or otherwise, try any or all of the following: cold water, saliva, kneadable putty eraser, MagicRub eraser, laundry soap, washing by hand, washing by machine, stain removers. Avoid using rusty pins, and never leave pins in your work. Beware of using bright or dark tacking (basting) thread; it can leave small fibres in the fabric which are virtually impossible to remove.

Chapter Three

TACKING, QUILTING AND FINISHING

TACKING (BASTING)

*I*f you are going to work on a portable frame, the three layers of the quilt need to be thoroughly tacked (basted) before you begin.

Insufficient tacking allows the layers to shift out of line as the frame is taken on and off the work. Tacking can be tedious and backbreaking, but it is important and should not be skimped. Many quilters prefer to spread the quilt layers out on the floor and wear their knees out. Lay out the backing on the floor, wrong side up, and smooth it out as much as possible. It may help to pin one edge to the carpet or tape it to the floor. Lay the wadding (batting) over the backing and smooth it out. Now lay the top down, right side uppermost and smooth it towards the edges; both the wadding and backing should extend beyond the edges of the quilt top about 4 inches (10 cm) on each side. Any less is risky, as the quilting process takes up and shrinks all three layers. Excess wadding and

backing can be trimmed away when the quilting is finished, but it is difficult to add extra!

If you feel that your knees are not tough enough to work on the floor, you can tack your quilt on a table and let your back take the strain! Almost any table will do, but highly-polished ones may get scratched. Table-tennis tables are ideal but any smooth clean surface can be used.

Spread the backing out on the table top, wrong side up, its centre in the middle of the table. Let the rest of the backing hang over the table edges. Centre the wadding in the same way and then position the quilt top over these two layers.

SEQUENCE FOR TACKING

Generally tacking is begun at the centre and worked out to the edges in an orderly and systematic fashion so all the

Tacking (basting) the layers of a quilt on a table

layers can be smoothed out to the edges as tacking progresses and any wrinkles are hopefully eliminated. If you are working on a table, tack from the centre outwards in both horizontal and vertical directions until you reach the edge of the table. Leave the threads dangling to continue tacking in the next stage. Now tack further horizontal and vertical lines, again working from the centre towards the table's edge (Figs 6a, b, c, and d).

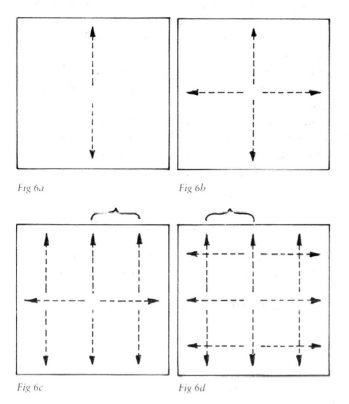

Fig 6a

Fig 6b

Fig 6c

Fig 6d

Once you have a tacked grid completed over the portion of quilt on the table top, slide this completed section out of the way, rethread the loose ends and continue tacking until there is a grid of tacked lines over the whole quilt. The optimum distance between tacking lines is 3 inches (7.5 cm).

Some instructions for tacking indicate diagonal lines worked immediately after the central horizontal and vertical lines, but on medium to large pieces it is possible to smooth the layers, unwittingly, out of true along the bias as you tack. The tacked grid just described is less likely to result in any such distortion.

Should you decide to work on the floor, tack either from the centre outwards or from one edge to the opposite. Smooth the layers out carefully and consistently towards the cut edges and there should be few problems.

You can use a traditional frame as an alternative to tacking on a table or floor. Ideally, the frame should be larger than the quilt so that all three layers can be stretched evenly, secured and then tacked, or you could use a frame with rollers. Secure the three layers to the near rail as if you were going to quilt; roll and tighten the backing in place on the far rail. The top two layers can then be smoothed, a little at a time, over the top of the taut backing and tacked in place, rolling the work on as required.

TACKING (BASTING) STITCH

The lines of tacking (basting) stitches ought to be reasonably straight, but it does not matter if they wobble slightly. To do their job of holding all three layers together, the stitches need to be neither too big nor too small, and moderately even. So loose stitches 6 inches (15 cm) long will not be suitable, nor will short tight stitches of 1 inch (2.5 cm).

You may find it helpful to use a spoon to make tacking easier. Push the layers down with the tip of the spoon just ahead of where the needle should emerge (Fig 7).

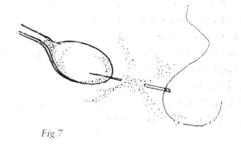

Fig 7

Avoid tacking too close to planned quilting lines – the tacking stitches will get in the way of the quilting.

The work may be more manageable if you roll up the tacked layers close to each line of tacking just completed.

To help keep the quilt edges clean and free from undue wear while you are quilting, fold the backing fabric over to the front of the quilt, enclosing the excess wadding and secure with loose tacking stitches.

Tacking thread should be visible on the quilt top. Dark or bright-coloured tacking thread is not suitable for pale fabrics, as tiny fibres from the thread can embed themselves in the top fabric and appear as small dots in the completed quilt after the tacking has been removed.

Needles for tacking Any needle that can be threaded with ease, preferably longer than a betweens, is fine for tacking. You may find it helpful to thread several needles in advance ready to use. An entire packet of needles can be threaded onto one reel or spool of quilting thread and pulled off singly as needed.

SETTING UP A TRADITIONAL FRAME

If you plan to quilt on a static frame, it is not necessary to tack the three quilt layers together before setting the quilt into the frame. Tack the backing fabric firmly to both rails, roll it out and stretch it smoothly. The wadding and top are then tacked to the near rail, smoothed out over the taut backing and left to hang over the far rail. A row of pins holds all three layers together in front of the far rail, and the sides of the quilt are tensioned by tapes pinned through all the layers of the edges and either pinned onto the webbing of the two stretchers or wound around the stretchers as in Fig 5, page 22.

QUILT-AS-YOU-GO

This is a great way of quilting something large in manageable sections. The technique is widely used for pieced and appliqué quilts and for machine quilting, but it is less appropriate for wholecloth quilts. Sections of the quilt are tacked, quilted and then joined together. Unless you work on a small traditional frame, you need to tack the three layers of each section together exactly as you would for a larger project. You will also need extra-generous seam allowances on all three layers of the quilt to provide sufficient unquilted fabric to join together.

When all the quilted sections have been completed, lay them out flat, reverse side uppermost. Fold back the wadding and backing so the top fabric can be matched up, pinned and seamed together (Fig. 8).

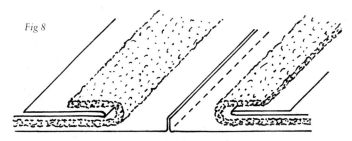

Fig 8

Trim the wadding and butt the pieces together with herringbone stitch (Fig 9).

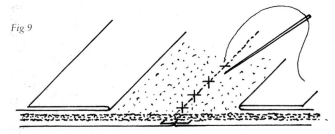

Fig 9

Then join the backing fabric by trimming and smoothing one raw edge and overlapping it with the folded edge of the second piece of backing. Stitch this folded edge neatly in place with matching thread (Fig 9a). Make sure that all joins are lapped in the same direction; they can be covered with straight tape if you wish.

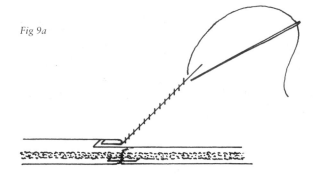

Fig 9a

Some quilters feel that this technique is fine for quilting small sections of a quilt, but find the assembly process slow because it requires precision planning.

HAND QUILTING

Quilting is a running stitch worked through layers of fabric and wadding. Its function is to hold these layers together and give texture. Running stitch is often the first one we learn and also the first we forget.

Good running stitches are even; both the stitches themselves and the spaces between appear to be the same length. Just for the moment, forget anything you have ever read or heard about size of stitch and concentrate on the word 'even'. If you are new to quilting, you should aim for even stitches, not small ones. Be realistic and take one step at a time. Like many skills, quilting requires practice and a little patience during the first stages – everyone feels 'all fingers and thumbs' to begin with.

Good hand quilting is worked with an evenly spaced running stitch through three layers of fabric. Each stitch should go through all three layers. Ideally, the stitches on the back should appear to be almost the same size as those on top. Heirloom-quality hand quilting shows all these things and also has a seemingly impossible number of stitches to the inch!

STARTING TO QUILT

Thread the needle before cutting an 18-inch (45-cm) length of thread. If you have difficulty in threading the needle, try turning the needle round or threading against a white or light background. Thread which has been cut diagonally rather than straight is easier to take through the eye of a fine needle. Longer threads often result in fraying and knotting (not to mention fraying of temper). Make a knot an inch or so away from the cut end. If you wax your thread, make a habit of removing excess wax or you may find an interesting number of small blobs on the top of your work. Run the thread across the beeswax and then between your thumb and forefinger. Take the needle down through the top and wadding only and bring

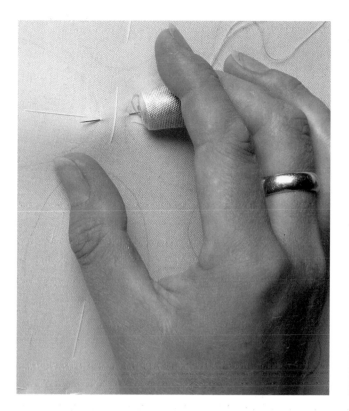

When starting to quilt, bring the needle out on the marked stitching line

The position of the knot when starting a new section of quilting

the needle back up through the top on the first line you are going to quilt.

Try to position both starting and finishing threads and knots so that they are either under an existing line of quilting or will have quilting worked over them. With pieced or appliqué tops, anchor starting and finishing threads and knots in the seam allowances wherever possible. If you are quilting a number of lines, try to stagger the starting and finishing points of each line so that they do not coincide.

Give a light tug on the thread; the knot should 'pop' through the top fabric and be hidden in the wadding. Begin your first line of quilting with a small backstitch through either the top two layers only (i.e. top and wadding) or through all three layers. You may, if you prefer, omit the backstitch so long as you feel confident that the knot is holding the thread securely. Now you are ready to proceed. The statement that quilting is a running stitch worked through three layers may now sound rather glib. How will you ever get that short needle through all three layers with any degree of evenness or accuracy? Holding the needle between thumb and forefinger is not very helpful – controlling the needle from the be-thimbled finger of your sewing hand is simpler, but requires a little perseverance to begin with.

The non-sewing hand should push up from underneath

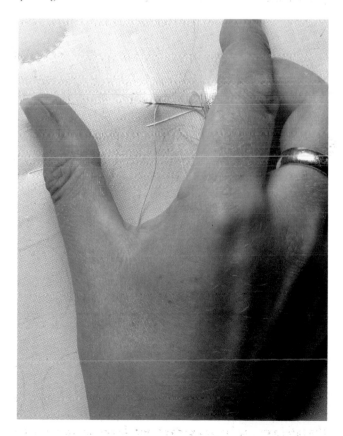

The position of the sewing hand on top of the quilt

at the stitching point and, by controlling rather than holding the needle, the thumb of the sewing hand is free to drop down just beyond the bump made underneath.

The compression of the quilt layers at this point makes it easier for the needle to penetrate all layers and to return to the top of the work.

So, hold the needle, push it down through all layers towards your non-sewing hand, (which should be pushing from underneath the layers towards you), drop the thumb of your sewing hand onto the quilt top and pray. You may find it helps to make a conscious effort to 'push' what remains of your sewing hand down towards the quilt at the same time as dropping your thumb and firmly pushing upwards with the underneath hand. Trying to describe the stages of this process is rather like describing an accordion without being able to move your hands! Now you see why we start with only even stitches as our aim. Don't agonise and analyse your first few stitches; take a few deep breaths and keep going. If you were at an art class, you would not expect to draw like Rembrandt in the first lesson! Gradually you will establish some sort of rhythm; experienced quilters speak of a rocking motion as typifying the hand movements of quilting.

IN MORE DETAIL

Hold the needle between your index finger and thumb to push it down through the layers, slide your thimble up behind the eye of the needle so that the top of the needle is firmly braced against either the side or the top of the thimble – whichever feels most natural. The thimble finger steadies the needle as the thumb drops down ahead of the needle point. A hill or bump will be made in the quilt from the upwards push of the underneath fingers. Drop the thumb in front of this bump to compress the layers and alter the axis of the hand. Both the fingers underneath and the thumb on top move along a little with each stitch; the thumb lifts and drops each time. At the beginning of the stitch the heel of the sewing hand rests on the work and, as the thumb drops down, the weight of the hand follows it, so that a shallow semi-circular wrist movement is described.

Push the needle through the layers with either the top or side of your thimble. It is possible with practice to roll your underneath finger out of the way of the downward needle once the point has grazed your fingertip.

After the thread is drawn through to complete the stitch(es), give a light tug to tension. This will help to seat the stitches firmly in place and gives better definition to the stitched line. Don't tug too hard or the thread will break.

While you grapple with all these instructions, may I plead with you not to keep turning your work over to inspect the back? The more you inspect, the more con-

scious you become of every missed stitch (and there is bound to be more than one). This just gives you something else to worry about and is counter-productive. One would-be quilter was taught to keep a mirror behind her work so she could check the back. She became so anxiety-ridden that her first quilt languished unfinished in a cupboard for more than a year. After an hour of sympathetic encouragement and reassurance that the mirror was unnecessary, she went home, dragged out the quilt and thoroughly enjoyed herself. Quilting is fun and therapeutic – take it slowly and allow plenty of time to learn and practice.

It is not always easy to make every stitch go through all three layers when you first start to quilt. Resist the urge to unpick every stitch. Eventually you will find that the majority of your stitches *will* go through all the layers with only the occasional 'missed' stitch on the reverse. Some experienced quilters say that the back of the work should be indistinguishable from the front. This may be the case with their own work, but you should keep your expectations realistic and achievable. If 75 per cent of your first stitches go through all three layers, you are doing extremely well and practice will bring improvement.

ONE STITCH AT A TIME

You may produce even stitches more easily by taking one stitch at a time. Making a single stitch and pulling all the thread through each time can be slow. The process can be speeded up if you pull the thread through only after taking several separate stitches, or load several stitches onto the needle as in ordinary running stitch. Work with single stitches if you find this comfortable – so long as the stitches are even it doesn't matter how they are achieved. Finding that you can take more than one stitch at a time is a wonderful feeling. There is no correct number of stitches to take on each needleful – some quilters take two or three; others take more than four. Again, it is the quality and evenness of the stitches that matters – the number is immaterial.

On tight curves it may be easier to take just one or two stitches at a time – straight lines are more encouraging for those who like to load their needles. Beware the first stitch if you develop into a multi-stitch quilter – it is easy enough to judge the evenness of the stitches loaded onto the needle, but even easier to misjudge the length of each beginning stitch, with the result that lines of quilting are punctuated with smaller, unattractive stitches.

QUILTING TIME

When you begin quilting, you will be concentrating hard and working at close quarters. After half an hour, get up and rearrange your neck and spine and refocus your eyes. Walk away from your chair and stretch a little and gaze out of the window. You will have been blissfully unaware that your shoulders were hunched and tense and that your blink rate had dropped, not to mention the tongue held elegantly between the teeth!

Are you sitting comfortably? Choose your quilting chair carefully – good back support will make all the different while you quilt, particularly if you will be working at a traditional frame. An adjustable office chair, or a 'kneeler' or back chair, offers the best support.

Please adjust your light Try to quilt in a good light. Daylight quilting is an ideal luxury, but many quilters tackle their work after a busy day. If you are quilting at night, make sure that you have ample light. General overhead lighting is not sufficient; move a lamp close to your chair. Having a good light on your work is less tiring on the eyes and will help you relax and enjoy your quilting. It can be very difficult to see yellow marks on white fabric under artificial light; use a different coloured marker if possible.

THE 'RIGHT' TENSION

If you try quilting without a frame or hoop, it is not too difficult to manipulate the layers onto the point of the needle as if you were working running stitch. Since a hoop or frame holds the layers flat, this manipulation is not possible, so try not to stretch the quilt layers drum-tight in the frame to begin with. There should be some 'give' to allow the non-sewing hand to push up from underneath. Some quilters like the work held loosely in the frame, others need considerable tension on the layers – experiment to find what works best for you.

MOVING AROUND

Now that you have begun to quilt, you will soon need either to finish off the thread or move from one part of the design to another. Moving is accomplished by 'floating', or taking the needle and thread down beneath the top fabric into and through the wadding and along to the next quilting line. Bring the needle back up through the top fabric, make a tiny backstitch through either the top two or all three layers and continue quilting. Depending on the distance between the lines of quilting, it may be necessary to float more than once.

If you need to float more than twice to reach the next line of quilting, finish off the thread and start again instead. If you are using a strong-coloured thread on pale fabrics, float as little as possible to prevent any show-through. Some quilters like to change the direction of quilting as often as possible, believing that this lessens the

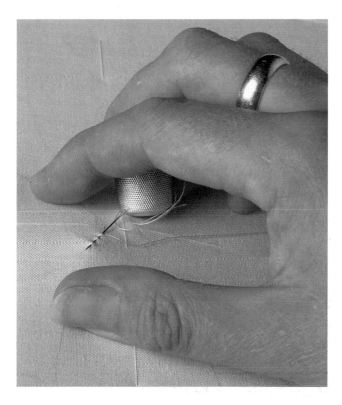

Drop the thumb to take it clear of the emerging needle. Notice the 'bump' made by the underneath hand as the thimble on the sewing hand pushes the needle through the quilt layers

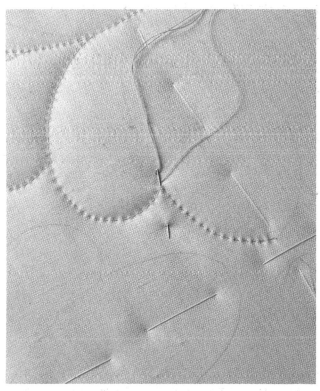

'Floating' the needle unseen through the wadding (batting) is the best way to move from one line of stitching to another

tension on the stitches and will result in fewer stitches breaking in the future.

FINISHING OFF

Finishing off the thread is broadly the reverse of the starting procedure. Make a tiny backstitch through two or three layers as before, then take the needle through the top fabric, along the wadding and return it to the surface. Try to position the thread underneath so more quilting will be worked over it, thus anchoring it even more firmly in place.

Now make a knot in the thread and 'pop' it down into the wadding. Bring the needle back through to the top again, leaving the knot in the wadding.

Clip the thread close to the top, pulling upwards as you clip so that the cut end will fall back beneath the top fabric. Keep the scissor blades horizontal and parallel with the work. Once you have clipped the thread, go back and clip the beginning tail of thread in the same way.

One way of eliminating some of the stopping and starting is as follows. Use twice the length of thread, say 36 inches (90 cm), leave half of this trailing on top of the work and begin to quilt. Finish off this half of the thread in the usual manner; return to the other half length and stitch in the opposite direction.

Finishing off the thread

Quilting is begun, worked and finished from the top. There should be no knots hanging from the back and no one should be able to tell where you have begun and ended or moved quilting lines.

SIZE OF STITCH

It is hard to understand why so many quilters feel that all quilting stitches should be small. Most teachers emphasise the importance of even stitching and encourage their students to concentrate on achieving just this. *Small stitches are not necessarily better.* It may reassure you to know that everyone's quilting stitch decreases slightly in size with practice and all quilters eventually arrive at a particular stitch length which is easy and comfortable for them. It is difficult to make very small quilting stitches which are also even – the majority of experienced quilters can make small stitches, but these often have spaces which are longer than the stitches themselves. If you make large even stitches, do not agonise over their size – instead be proud that they are even. (Fig 10 shows some of the possible stitch variations.)

Be prepared to change needles frequently if you are working in warm conditions. Needles tarnish and become blunt, particularly if you use a thimble on your underneath finger.

Fig 10

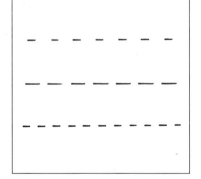

UNPICKING/RIPPING OUT

Perfectionist quilters say that they unpick almost as many stitches as they make. Constant unpicking is counterproductive – you may soon become expert at unpicking, but not an expert quilter. Frequent pauses for unpicking also prevent you from developing the rhythm that is so important if your quilting is to improve. No one is suggesting that you adopt a careless attitude to your work, just remember that it is possible to be over-anxious.

Straight-line patterns should be accurately measured either before or during quilting. If some of the *stitches* are not absolutely straight, this will not show in the finished piece unless you are working with miniature scale. On the other hand, if entire lines are distinctly wobbly or out of true with each other, they should probably be unpicked and adjusted. Several slight flaws in the quilting will be less obvious than one large one. Restrict yourself to unpicking only major errors. If you must unpick, use the eye of your needle rather than the point – there is less likelihood of splitting or fraying the thread this way.

Stab stitch comes into its own when you cannot avoid stitching through several seam allowances and it is almost impossible to make a running stitch. As a general rule, stab stitch does not give a neat result on the reverse side, but many quilters produce exquisite work with this method. Because each stitch is worked in two distinct movements, the stab technique is slightly slower than running stitch, but good results can be obtained if the layers are stretched taut, which helps keep the stitches straight on the reverse. Most quilting teachers prefer their students to master running stitch, but if this method really does not suit you, experiment with stab stitching.

QUILTING SEQUENCE

Plan to quilt systematically. If you are using a traditional frame, you will begin at one edge, quilt along the length of the frame and roll the quilt on until you reach the far edge. So long as you don't jump from one section to another, you should obtain perfectly good results if you start with your hoop or frame in one corner, work along one edge and then return to the beginning corner again to continue (Fig 11a). Any slight movement then occurs consistently in the same direction.

Fig 11a

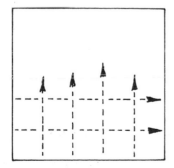

The drawback to the general advice to begin in the centre is that first stitches will be of lesser quality. Everyone's quilting improves during the making of a quilt, so by starting at one edge, any differences in stitching should be less noticeable.

Working main pattern lines and background together, rather than starting with the pattern and returning to the background later, will give a crisper, smoother finish. It is possible to work pattern first and background second – and sometimes the choice of background quilting is made after the main patterns have been quilted – but

guard against little tucks creeping in where one line of quilting meets another.

In quilting background lines, best results seem to be obtained from stitching in the same direction (Fig 11b), rather than turning and stitching the next line in the opposite direction (Fig 11c). It may seem more economical to turn back, but it can cause a slight diagonal shifting of the fabric between the quilted lines which can be quite noticeable on fabrics with a lustrous finish.

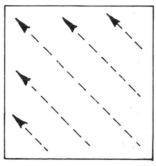 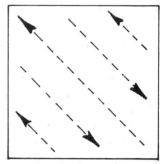

Fig 11b *Fig 11c*

If possible avoid crossing stitches where lines of quilting intersect. If this involves an unusually long gap between stitches, float the thread through the wadding rather than have an extra-long stitch showing on the reverse.

Crosshatching A simple, fairly quick way of working crosshatch lines on a traditional frame is either to stitch away from the near rail and leave the needle or thread to be picked up later, or to stitch to a comfortable distance away, anchoring the thread with a small backstitch, and continue back towards you so that a right angled line has been formed (Fig 12).

Fig 12

Borders It may be easier to quilt a particularly narrow border after the raw edges have been neatened. Otherwise, if you are working on a portable hoop or frame, tack (baste) a length of old towel to the raw edges and stitch as close to the border edges as required.

Pre-printed panels There is no shame in using pre-printed panels for quilting practice; these blocks are often an ideal introduction to all the quilting processes except marking out a pattern. Panels can be quilted as little or as much as personal taste dictates. The most important thing about these panels is that a beginner's stitches tend to 'get lost' in the texture. Even if individual stitches do show, the results still look attractive.

You can use these panels as practice stitching pieces, or keep a practice piece made from plain fabric in a small frame marked up with different backgrounds to use for establishing a rhythm before stitching on something more important. It could be a cushion in a small frame that you work on before you quilt a full-size masterpiece. You can be more productive and improve the quality of your stitching at the same time!

Other ways of holding the needle There are few absolutes in quilting – the manner, direction and execution of the stitch is a matter of choice. Many quilters work horizontally from right to left (left-handers work in reverse). If you watch a 'traditional' quilter at work, you may notice that the direction of stitches is away from the body, using the forefinger and not the thumb to push down the fabric ahead of the needle. It is worth experimenting to see which method feels most comfortable and natural to you.

BINDING AND FINISHING

This final process of quiltmaking can considerably enhance your work. Take a little time to decide which finish will be best for your quilt. All quilts suffer a good deal of wear and tear at their edges, so attention to finishing is important. There are five main ways of finishing a quilt. For best results with all methods use a thread which matches the binding fabric rather than the main body of the quilt.

BACK TO FRONT

A very successful way of finishing a quilt is to bring the backing fabric over to the front and slip stitch it into position. This gives the appearance of a binding and is easy to do, but there must be sufficient surplus backing fabric to begin with.

A single line of quilting worked close to the edge of the 'binding' will help to give a good finish and keeps the layers stable as you complete the edging. Work this line of quilting at the measured depth of the 'binding' from the raw edge of the top fabric.

Once all the quilting is complete, trim the edges of both top and wadding (batting) so that they are flush with each other. On the reverse side of the quilt, measure and mark from the final line of quilting a depth of three times the 'binding' depth plus seam allowances and cut away the surplus (Fig 13a).

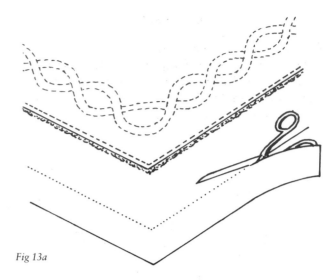

Fig 13a

Next fold the raw edges of the backing in to meet the raw edges of the top and wadding. Finger press as you go along. The folded outside edge of the backing can now be brought over to the front of the quilt and pinned into position (Fig 13b).

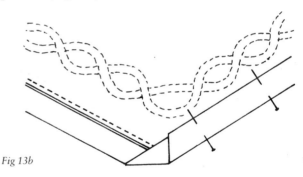

Fig 13b

Leave the final line of quilting just visible. Make sure that you do not inadvertently pull the folded fabric out of place, or the finished edges will not lie as flat as they should. Folding the backing will make the 'binding' feel more substantial and prevent the top fabric from showing through a dark top with pale backing. It is also easier and more accurate to pin and stitch a folded edge than to turn the raw edges under as you stitch. Slip hem just above the line of quilting using a thread which matches the top fabric (Fig 13c).

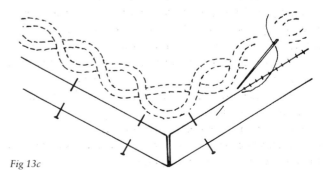

Fig 13c

CORNERS

If you have been careful in measuring and trimming the backing fabric, it will be fairly easy to fold at the corners to form a mitre (Fig 13d). Trim away the corner to reduce bulk if you wish. Stitch the folded edges of each mitre together to secure the fold (Fig 13e).

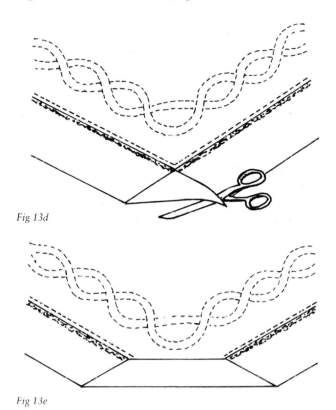

Fig 13d

Fig 13e

If there is insufficient backing to fold down to the raw edges of top and wadding, neaten the raw edges of the backing with a narrow machine hem or pin or tack a narrow hem on the backing before bringing it over to the front. A machined hem can be turned under again from the front to hide the line of machine stitching – tacking or pins will need to be removed as the backing is stitched.

FRONT TO BACK

This way of finishing quilt edges is less popular than bringing the back over to the front. The finished single folded edge does not look so substantial or complete, but a final line of quilting, as described above, will help.

You may prefer to turn the front fabric over to the back if you feel that the colour or print of the backing fabric would detract from the quilt if it were visible from the front as a 'binding'.

The method is the same as outlined above, but it is the top fabric which is measured, trimmed and folded over to the back and hemmed into place.

EDGES TO MIDDLE

This popular and easy way to finish quilt edges, particularly successful on wholecloth quilts, involves folding both top and backing fabrics in to meet each other (Fig 14a).

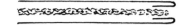

Fig 14a

Trim and level any excess wadding so that it does not protrude beyond these folded edges. Pin or tack the layers of fabric together as you fold them in. Work one line of running stitches through all the layers very close to the folded edges and then a second line of running stitches a short distance away (Fig 14b). Use the same thread as that already used for the quilting.

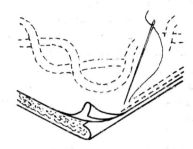

Fig 14b

This method of finishing can be seen on many old quilts, often with lines of machine stitching rather than running stitch. A machine-finished edge was considered superior in strength and durability to hand finishing. Also, at a time when sewing machines were a status symbol, a machine-finished quilt indicated ownership of this coveted item! You can machine the edges if you wish, but some lightweight machines may not cope with the thickness of the folded fabrics.

BINDING

Binding gives an excellent and versatile finish for pieced and appliquéd quilts. Bindings can contrast or blend with the main fabrics or accentuate one of the colours.

The quality of ready-made bindings is not usually good enough to use for quilts. Making your own binding offers greater flexibility both in colour choices and fabric quality.

Single binding is the most economical. Calculate the width of the binding by adding together the depth of binding you wish to show on the front and the back, plus two seam allowances for hemming on each side. Cut the binding fabric on the straight grain, preferably in unjoined lengths. If you need to join binding strips together, plan it so the seams occur halfway along the finished length, not near the corners or at irregular intervals. With the right side of the binding facing the right side of the quilt top, machine into place with a ¼ inch (0.6 cm) seam allowance (Fig 15a). (Use a long stitch and slacken the tension slightly to allow for the extra thickness you will be stitching through).

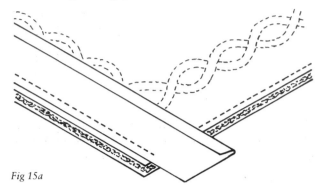

Fig 15a

Turn under the binding seam allowance and bring it over to the reverse side of the quilt so that it just touches the line of machining. Hem or slip hem the binding into position through the machine stitches to prevent any stitches from being visible on the top of the quilt (Fig 15b).

Fig 15b

Corners can be worked as shown (Fig 15c) by overlapping the strips and turning under the last raw edges to neaten them before finally stitching into place.

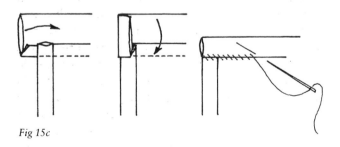

Fig 15c

Continuous bias binding Pre-joined lengths of bias binding can be made from a square of fabric. Cut the square of fabric into two equal right-angled triangles (Fig

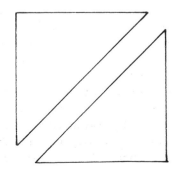

Fig 16a

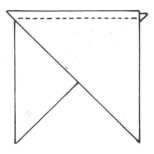

Fig 16b

16a) and rejoin them to make a parallelogram (Fig 16b). Press the seam open. Measure and mark out the width of strip required and join the angled ends of the parallelogram together to form a cylinder, offsetting the marked strips (Figs 16c and d).

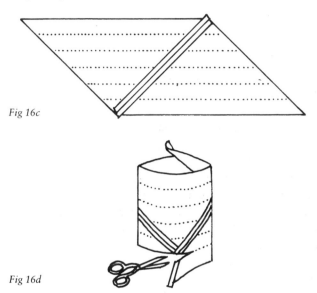

Fig 16c

Fig 16d

Press this last seam open before beginning to cut along the marked lines. This method for cutting continuous lengths of bias binding can be used for either single or double binding.

Double binding (French fold) means that there are two thicknesses of fabric binding your quilt, which is both firmer and more substantial than single binding (Fig 17a).

Figh 17a

Double binding can be cut either on the straight grain or on the bias. Bias binding is perhaps easier to handle around curved edges and corners. Straight edge quilts should have a straight grain binding to avoid any stretching or rippling of the quilt edges.

To calculate the width of strip to cut for a double binding, measure the depth you want to show on the top of the quilt. Multiply this by four and add on a generous

½ inch (1.3 cm). Mark out, then cut strips of this width from the binding fabric. The cut strips are then folded in half, wrong sides together, with raw edges matching, and pressed. Take care when pressing bias fabric – press down with the iron rather than moving it from side to side, which could distort the strips. The quilt layers should have any excess trimmed away so that all the edges are flush. Position and pin the folded strips on the top of the quilt so that the raw edges of both quilt and binding are aligned as in Fig 17b.

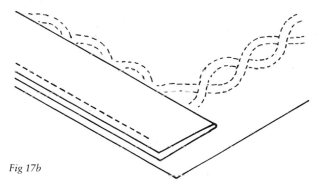

Fig 17b

The strips can be sewn in place through all layers, either by hand or machine. Machine-stitching makes a good firm line and is quicker. Keep a generous and consistent ½ inch (1.3 cm) from the raw edges. Once the binding has been attached to the quilt, fold it over to the back so that the folded edge of the binding just shows the line of stitching. The binding is then slipstitched in place using a matching thread.

Corners can be made in the same way as for single binding. Work along each side, overlapping and hemming the strips at the corners. However, neatly mitred corners are easy and add a very professional touch. Join your binding strips into one continuous length measuring the same as the perimeter of the quilt with a generous allowance for corners before folding the strips. Position the folded binding at the midpoint of one side and pin in place. When a corner is reached, pin at the exact spot where the two seam allowances will meet (Fig 18a).

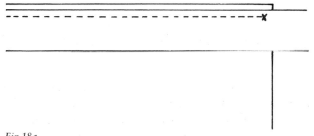

Fig 18a

Now take the binding strip to the left so that a 45° fold is made and the unattached strip is to the left of this fold (Fig 18b).

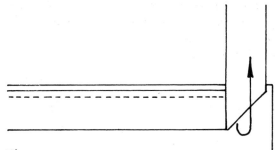

Fig 18b

Pin along the 45° fold and then bring the unattached strip back over to the right to cover this pinned fold. After making the 45° fold, bring the binding straight down, matching all raw edges (Fig 18c).

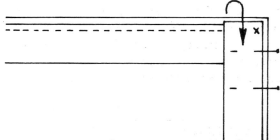

Fig 18c

The top fold should line up with the edge of the binding – or in the case of a wide binding, the fold should be in line on the left with the depth of the finished binding (any less and the mitre will not lie flat on the reverse side.) Keep the raw edges of the strip aligned with the quilt edges. Machine the binding into place. When you reach a corner, stop on the spot and fold to make the mitre before continuing. This helps to correct any errors which would mean unpicking a long line of stitching. Continue to pin the strip along the next edge, folding and pinning in the same way at each of the corners. Stitch, by hand or machine, through all layers of both binding and quilt, and remove pins as you go. At the corners, stitch only to the point where the seam allowances meet and finish off securely. Begin stitching again from this same point on the uppermost binding strip and continue to the next corner. When all the binding is in place, it can be turned over to the back so that the folded edge just touches the line of stitching and then hemmed in place. The corners on both back and front should fold together into neat mitres. Practise with some scraps of fabric first – it is not as complicated as it sounds.

If you want a double binding but have insufficient fabric, the following 'dodge' may help. Calculate the depth of the binding front and back plus two seam allowances for fabric A (top fabric) and fabric B (lining fabric). Mark and cut out. Place the strips of fabric A and

B with right sides together and seam together. Press the seam open. If the binding and lining fabrics (A and B) have had to be joined to make continuous strips, try to avoid having these seams directly on top of each other as this creates too much bulk. The new strip is then folded exactly on this seam line, wrong sides together, and the binding attached to the quilt as described above. All this requires extra measuring and seaming, but can be a lifesaver if you are faced with too little fabric to make a double binding.

PIPING

Piped, or corded, edges for a quilt can look very elegant. Piping cord is available in a variety of thicknesses – medium is usually a good choice for a large quilt; the finer grades are more suitable for small projects. The best piping cord is polyester since, unlike cotton, it requires no pre-shrinking.

Cut bias fabric strips wide enough to enclose the cord and leave a generous ½ inch (1.3 cm) seam allowance. Fold the strip over the cord, with the right side showing and stitch very close to the cord using a toning thread (Fig 19a). A zipper foot allows you to stitch much closer to the cord than a presser foot.

Fig 19a

You can attach the piping to the quilt top before assembling the layers; the single layer is not so bulky.

The covered piping is then pinned in position on the quilt top with its raw edges to the outside edge (Fig 19b).

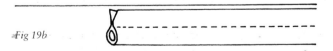

Fig 19b

After stitching the piping in place through the quilt top only, both excess wadding and quilt top can be trimmed flush with the raw edges of the piping. These raw edges are then turned to the middle of the quilt's thickness and the backing is folded over to enclose the raw edges, just covering the machined line on the piping (Fig 19c).

Fig 19c

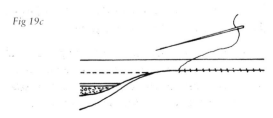

Slip stitch the folded backing in place on the piping using thread to match the backing. To complete the piping splice and secure the cord (Fig 19d) and overlap the covering fabric.

Fig 19d

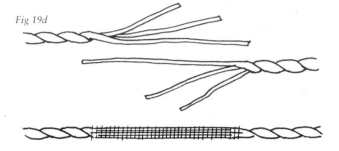

Thick and thin piping Once you are familiar with basic piping, you might like to enhance a quilt with a double piped edge. Cover two separate cords of differing thickness with fabrics which accentuate the colours of the quilt top. The cords are covered individually and machined together before being attached to the top of the quilt in the same way as single piping. Ready-made fine piping is available in a choice of colours including gold and silver.

Soft piping Substitute a strip of wadding for piping cord to produce a soft rounded finish for a quilt.

PROJECT: 'TUDOR ROSE' CUSHION

Quilted cushion cover 12 inches (30 cm) square

YOU WILL NEED

16 in. (40 cm) square of top fabric
16 in. (40 cm) square of 2 oz. wadding (batting)
16 in. (40 cm) square of backing fabric
Fabric for back of cushion – allow a 20 in. (50 cm) square
Cushion pad 12 in. (30 cm) square
Betweens needles of your choice
Sewing/quilting thread to match top fabric
Tacking (basting) thread
Hoop or frame (optional)
Beeswax (optional)
16 in. (40 cm) square of tracing paper
Medium black felt marker pen, pencil, masking tape
Fabric marker (remember to test for removal)
Scissors, thimble

1 Press both top and backing fabric. Lightly mark centre of top fabric and set aside.

2 Mark centre of tracing paper square and line up with the match marks of the design on page 42, Fig 20.

Trace this quarter of the pattern using a black felt marker. Turn the tracing and complete the three remaining quarters of the design, marking the centre lines of the design as you trace. This tracing is now your Master Sheet.

3 If you are using a pale fabric, tape the Master Sheet onto a clean smooth surface. A sheet of white paper underneath will help you to see the lines more clearly when tracing through the fabric. Lay the top fabric over the Master Sheet, matching up the centre lines of the Master Sheet with those on the fabric. Smooth and tape the fabric into place.

4 Using your fabric marker, trace lightly over the pattern lines onto the top fabric, taking care not to press too hard.

Once the complete pattern is traced out, remove the tape from both fabric and Master Sheet.

5 If the top fabric is too dark to trace through, tape the Master Sheet and fabric to a sunny window and use a light-coloured marker to trace the design.

6 Lay the square of backing fabric out on a smooth surface, wrong side uppermost.

Position the wadding (batting) over the backing fabric, then lay the marked top fabric over the top.

7 Tack (baste) the three layers together, using a neutral coloured thread and working from the centre out to the edges in sequence. Smooth the layers out as you tack, checking that there are no wrinkles or puckers.

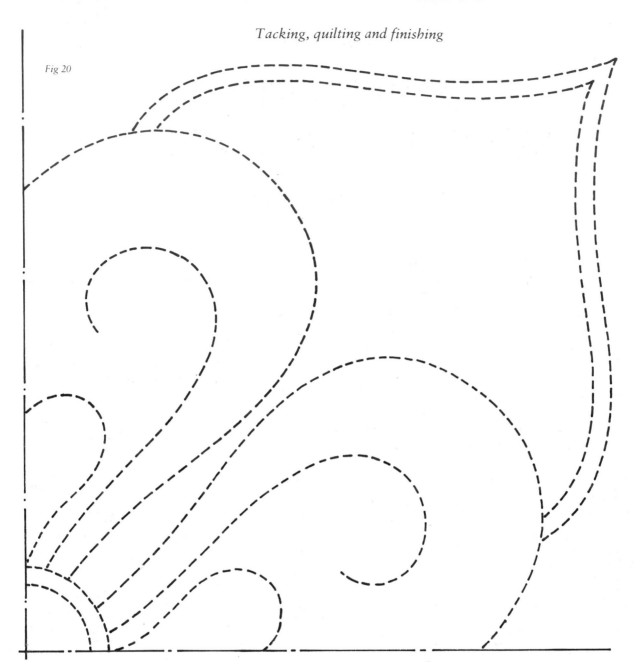

Fig 20

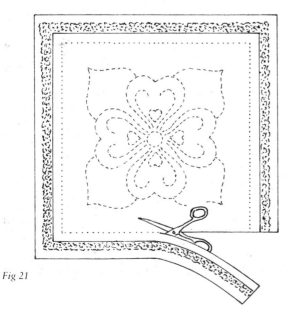

Fig 21

8 If you are using a portable hoop or frame, position the tacked sandwich so that the design is centred in the frame.

9 Begin quilting at the centre of the design or from one corner (see page 35) and continue systematically until the design is complete. Remember to remove the work from the frame when you are not quilting.

10 Once quilting is complete, remove all tacking stitches and any markings as necessary.

11 Measure and mark four lines 12 inches (30 cm) from the centre. These will be your seam lines for making up the cushion.

Trim away the excess from all three layers to within ¾ inch (2 cm) of these marked lines (Fig 21).

12 With the cushion back fabric, make up into a cushion cover using your preferred method.

Chapter Four

QUILTING, PATCHWORK AND APPLIQUÉ

Quilting stands as a technique on its own. Patchwork and appliqué are enhanced by quilting, and very few pieces of patchwork and appliqué are totally unsuitable subjects for quilting. It is merely a matter of selecting the most likely and often the simplest patterns. If you are feeling hesitant, a good general rule is to quilt simple lines which either contrast with, or complement, the main patterns.

If, for instance, an appliqué pattern is very strong and graphic, a closely worked background with 'character' quilting (see the photograph on page 47) on and around the appliqué shapes usually works very well. Similarly,

where it is important to keep the emphasis on the geometric shapes of strongly coloured and contrasting patchwork blocks, simple outline quilting and fairly close background quilting will look good.

Say you have a pieced or appliqué top to quilt which is made up of blocks set together edge to edge or with sashing strips of fabric in between. Plan to quilt the outlines of the main pattern shapes first. If the blocks are

Antique American quilt c. 1860 with appliqué top. The strong pattern is enhanced by the background quilting. (Quilt courtesy of Patricia Cox)

Each block in this Ocean Waves quilt has been stitched with a different quilting pattern

joined by sashing, quilt very close along both sides of the seam. This may give the effect you want. There may be a lot of unquilted space within the blocks themselves which could be filled with a background quilting pattern. A simple way of doing this is to mark straight lines with masking tape. These lines can all follow the same direction (Fig 22a), rotate within each block (Fig 22b) or radiate out from the centre of the block (Fig 22c). Crosshatching and pairing of lines are other possibilities.

Consider clamshell (see Fig 53a, page 78) or wineglass pattern (see Fig 53c, page 78) as a contrast if you feel straight lines of quilting are too similar to the angular edges of patchwork. So long as the scale and proportion of the background quilting remains fairly constant, you can even experiment with different background patterns for each block.

The humble straight line has much to contribute to the final appearance of any quilt, especially one which features appliqué. Don't be too anxious to fill wide open spaces with lots of different patterns. Most straight line quilting in this context will give the finished quilt a traditional look, but it has the advantage of being easy to mark (either with a ruler or tape) and the stitching seems to go quickly because you are not constantly changing direction. Also, quilting straight lines improves technique by allowing you to develop a rhythm.

Straight line quilting choices for the main or central background on an appliqué quilt could be any of the following:

Single, double or triple parallel lines running vertically (Figs 22d, e, and f).

Single, double or triple parallel lines running diagonally in one direction only (Figs 22g and h).

Single, double or triple parallel lines running diagonally changing direction in each quarter (as in Fig 22a).

Single, double or triple parallel lines running diagonally from the centre towards each corner (as in Fig 22c).

Single, double or triple lines crossing at right angles to form straight squares (Fig 22i and j).

Single, double or triple lines crossing at right angles to form squares 'on point' – otherwise known as waffle, grid or crosshatching (Figs 22k and l).

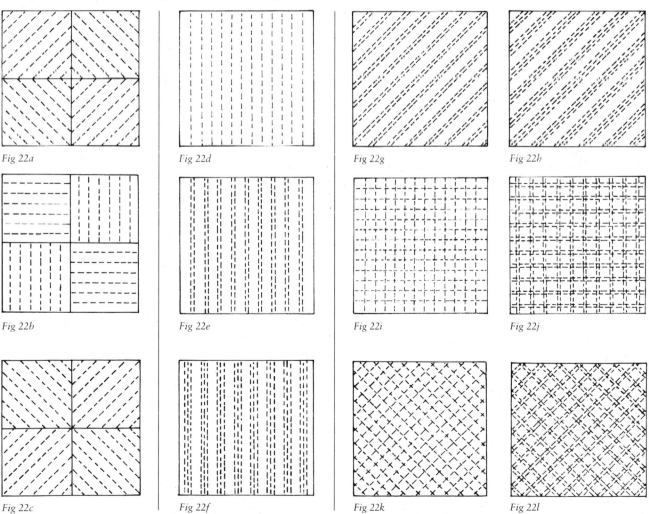

Fig 22a

Fig 22d

Fig 22g

Fig 22h

Fig 22b

Fig 22e

Fig 22i

Fig 22j

Fig 22c

Fig 22f

Fig 22k

Fig 22l

Remember – motifs used at random and wrongly sized can look splodgy and too isolated. There needs to be an overall evenness of texture (Fig 23).

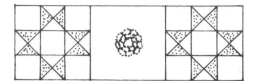

Fig 23

It is important not to produce a cluttered effect by using quilting patterns which demand serious attention in their own right; these will almost certainly detract from the main design. If there is a lot of open space between the main shapes and/or in the borders, feathered wreaths or the running feather patterns on page 105 will look striking. Feathers and floral appliqué shapes mix well in traditional settings, but are not the only combinations possible.

Many appliqué patterns, both traditional and contemporary, benefit from 'character' quilting; that is, lines of quilting worked over applied shapes to add detail. For instance, appliqué leaves can have quilted veins, and shading of flower petals can be suggested with short lines of quilting.

With the exception of folded and pressed patchwork techniques such as Folded Star, Suffolk Puffs (Yo-yos), Cathedral Window (Mayflower) and some Log Cabin, quilting can greatly enhance and enrich patchwork. Movement can be suggested by superimposing swirling curved lines on or near stark geometric shapes. Close quilting enriches and subtly alters colour. Emphasis of the main shapes can be increased by judicious use of outline or 'in the ditch' quilting, and seam lines between blocks can be minimised.

OUTLINE QUILTING

Most patchwork and appliqué looks best if it is first outlined with quilting. Outlining on patchwork can be done 'in the ditch', i.e., very close to, or actually on, the seams, or ¼ inch (0.6 cm) away from the seams. Appliqué shapes can also be defined with a line of quilting right next to the edge or a short distance away. Outline quilting emphasises the main patterns before other texture is added.

Outline quilting can be developed into echo quilting, which makes an effective setting for many appliqué patterns, especially when there are only a few blocks to be quilted as in the block opposite. This density of quilting would be rather time-consuming to work over a large quilt, but you might like to try it on a smaller scale, perhaps with a wallhanging or cushion.

ENHANCING PATCHWORK

Take care when deciding on quilting to enhance patchwork. As with appliqué, the quilting itself should not dominate or confuse by introducing too many diverse pattern elements.

Look at the Ohio Star quilt on page 49. Each block has been quilted in a slightly different way, from the most basic outline quilting to close parallel lines. The effect of a strong curling line is shown in the photographs. The contrast between the straight lines of the stars and the curves of the quilting, together with the sharp colour contrast, is bold and effective.

ALLOVER PATTERNS

Consider using an allover quilting pattern for your patchwork or appliqué. This gives a satisfying 'old fashioned' look, particularly where many different patterns or blocks have been combined, as in a sampler quilt. If your top is made of many small pieces such as diamonds or hexagons, it may be easier to quilt an allover pattern than to outline each individual shape. The quilt shown here shows an overlapping circle pattern sometimes referred to as Baptist Fan (Fig 24). Relatively quick and easy to mark out and quilt, this pattern is found on many American utility quilts.

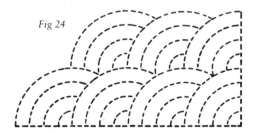

Fig 24

Other patterns, usually reserved for backgrounds, can be expanded for allover use. For example, wineglass, crosshatching and parallel lines all have a unifying effect. Generally, the quilting on appliqué tops should be chosen to enhance and contrast with the applied shapes in a subdued way. With patchwork tops the quilter is faced with almost too many choices and possibilities; the Ohio Star (page 62) gives a hint of this embarrassment of riches.

CHOOSING A PATTERN

One starting point for visualising quilting on a top, either patchwork or appliqué, is to use masking or drafting tape. Put strips of tape onto the quilt top to indicate where

Close echo quilting around a traditional oak-leaf pattern

Ohio Star 'sampler': a different motif in each block

quilting lines would be and then stand back and see if you like the effect. This is an excellent way of deciding how wide crosshatched lines should be, what paired parallel lines would look like, the impact of diagonal lines, radiating lines, and so on. Of course, quilted lines will look far more subtle than strips of tape, but this method can be most helpful if you reach that crisis of indecision which strikes all quilters from time to time. Another visual aid is chalk. Used lightly, this can help you to see how well the pattern fits the space and how it relates to the pieced or appliquéd shapes, and it can be brushed off fairly easily afterwards.

Before choosing any quilting patterns, remember that most patchwork and appliqué looks best with outline quilting around the main shapes to emphasise and define without detracting from the texture produced by further quilting. You may find outline quilting slightly tedious – you have already pieced or appliquéd the shapes that create these lines and the extra layers of seam allowances are not always easy to quilt through. Unless you quilt an

Ohio Star quilt, red stars on a blue background, made by Jane Arthur

allover pattern, such as might be needed for an abstract or landscape piece, some basic outline quilting is almost essential. Background or other quilting alone will not give the subtle emphasis that outlining will.

Quilt tops which offer most scope for enhancement by quilting are those with pieced or appliqué blocks separated by alternating plain blocks, and which have border spaces. If the quilt top is made up of blocks set directly edge to edge, or with narrow sashings, the only open spaces are those which form the background of each block. This does not limit you just to outline quilting; again, looking at the Ohio Star sample above; there is a variety of possibilities to choose from.

Aim for a similar proportion of quilted areas over the top as a whole. Large unquilted spaces next to small areas of close texture on the same piece will look unbalanced.

Blocks with outline quilting look best next to alternating blocks with a simple quilting design which fills the space as in Fig 25.

Fig 25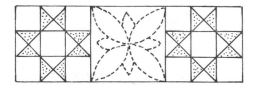

49

'Sugar loaf' scrap quilt, made in Texas c. 1870

If you are working with plain blocks or areas on the quilt top, looking at some easy possibilities may help you focus your ideas. Try repeating the outline of the block in the blank space; this shows the major shapes as texture, not as coloured shapes. If the pattern block is made up of quite large, simple shapes, the quilting in the alternate

Fig 25a

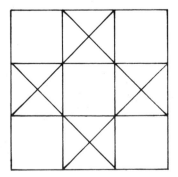

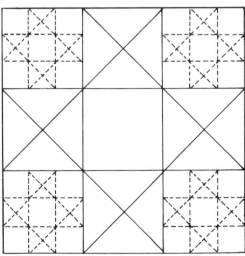

Fig 25b

blocks could be a reduction of the block pattern itself repeated, say, four times (Fig 25a and b).

Quilting lines can be drawn to connect the seam lines of the blocks to create a secondary pattern.

There may even be enough background space within the pattern block to allow a quilting pattern to be carried over from the adjacent block. This will minimise the seam lines most effectively.

Ordinary crosshatch or waffle quilting gives plenty of texture in return for few decisions – try to strike a balance between the spacing of the crosshatched lines and the unquilted spaces in the main block.

This sampler quilt made by Rosemary Wilde uses Ohio Star, Fan and Dresden Plate blocks enhanced by freehand quilting

50

Random curved or curling lines can be great fun to draw freehand and also to quilt. One student found that this was her preferred solution for filling the spaces in the central area of her first sampler-type quilt. She had used a strictly limited range of fabrics, and the striped, mitred frames of the individual blocks and borders added good definition. The quilting needed to provide plenty of texture and a little subtle contrast without distracting too much from the blocks and their setting. Eventually she felt brave enough to draw 'squiggles' freehand directly onto the fabric, without any particular plan. For a first attempt at a large-scale piece, the results are more than creditable and have increased her confidence enormously.

QUILTING SHAPES

A shape used in the piecing or appliqué could be adapted and developed into a quilting pattern. Extra leaves, flowers and buds can be quilted onto an appliqué block to make it look more complex, and a scaled-down Ohio Star can be quilted in each of the four corners of a large Ohio Star block (Fig 25b, page 50).

On the Roman Stripe quilt on page 54, the simple style and shapes of the patchwork were reflected in the choice of quilting pattern. The main background area was divided into triangles and filled with single parallel lines which referred to the strip piecing of the coloured triangles and continued the lines of the overall pieced design.

Note how the changes of direction of the quilting lines alter the perception of the black fabric, rather like the nap or sheen on velvet.

Complicated quilting patterns will not show clearly on a busy, close-printed fabric. Use simple patterns instead.

Curved line quilting patterns contrast well with the angles of pieced work – again, aim to balance the proportions and spacing of the quilting with that of the patchwork.

Block patterns with strong diagonal lines can be echoed in alternate blocks to carry through the general theme. Conversely, a horizontal/vertical, or cruciform, quilting pattern may contrast and balance equally well.

SMOOTHING THE ROUGH

There is one excellent reason for taking care with the quilting plan of any top and aiming at more than basic outline quilting. Many tops perversely refuse to lie smooth and flat with all seams meeting perfectly – and some resemble a major volcanic eruption! If this happens, do not despair. Much of this excess can be 'quilted out'

– that is, the tops can be made to look a lot better than they really are. This improvement process begins when you refuse to be beaten by inaccuracies of stitching, glaring or otherwise, and work a high density of quilting over the whole top. The quilting process allows you to make slight adjustments and realignments (alternatively called stretching and pushing into place) of the pattern pieces as you quilt around their outlines. Also, lots of quilting can, almost magically, make bulges and billows of fabric less apparent; sometimes (see below) they disappear altogether.

The small quilt shown here is a good example. More

The jointly made Double Wedding Ring quilt before quilting (below left); the layers have been tacked (basted), but will not lie flat. Below, the same quilt 'after'; the irregularities that occurred in the heat of the race have been 'quilted out'

than twenty individuals raced each other to hand stitch small sections of the Double Wedding Ring pattern. Much hilarity, and just a little lack of attention to the finer points of hand piecing, were the order of the hour. Assembling the results was accomplished with much frustration – no amount of pulling and pressing would make the top lie flat. Instead of consigning it to the back of a cupboard, they decided to prove the old quilters' maxim 'It'll quilt out'. As you can see from the completed quilt, this is just what happened. True, the piecing still lacks accuracy, but the overall effect is acceptable. So take heart if your piecing skills are not all you would like them to be – plenty of quilting can disguise this fact, and you can indeed fool some of the people some of the time!

Detail of a Roman Stripe quilt with parallel quilting

BORDERS

Thoughtfully planned and executed borders greatly improve the appearance of any quilt. The space available for quilting depends on the piecing or appliqué patterns and the construction of the border or borders. Again, the chosen quilting patterns should fill the space well and enhance the main body of the quilt. There is no need to hunt out specific border patterns – it is quite easy to devise your own by adapting the patterns or style of quilting already planned for the central areas (see Chapter Eight). Suppose you have chosen a pattern based on simple ovals for the alternating blocks and spaces. Many different patterns can be developed from this one shape and adapted to fit any width border (Fig 26). Use the mirror technique described on page 117 to help you turn corners or develop the patterns further.

If you are overwhelmed at the thought of planning borders, you may find it helpful and reassuring to work on strips of shelf paper first. This way, you can change your mind, and the drawn lines, as many times as you like without having to remove marks from the quilt top. You can also be certain that the chosen pattern will fit the space, have the right number of full repeats and turn corners neatly before you mark the quilt itself.

Cut strips of paper and tape them together to the exact size and length of the borders. Mark the midpoint – it will be useful if you decide to reverse the pattern here. Also mark the centre line along the length. Fold the paper strip into equal sections and/or match it up with the block seam lines, depending on the construction of the main part of the quilt. These fold lines form the framework for the border design (Fig 27).

If the border pattern is based on repeats of a single motif, the fold lines will help you make evenly spaced and balanced repeats. You can also check that the scale of the motif fits into the depth of the border, and make any

Fig 26

Fig 27

55

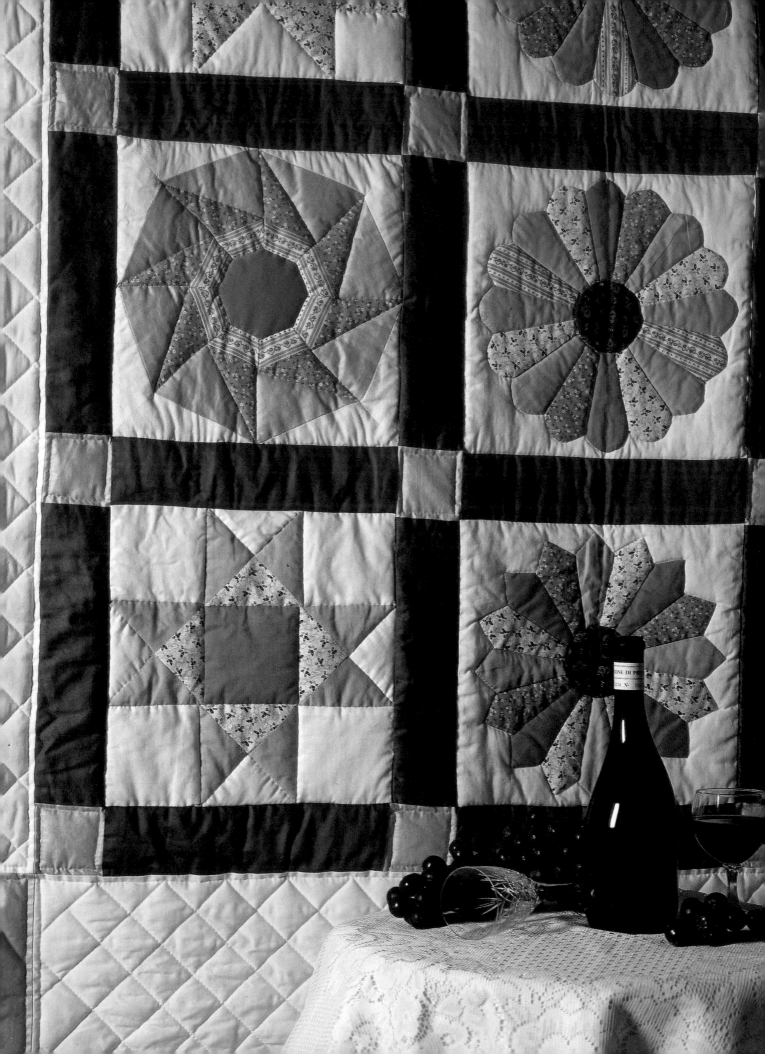

necessary adjustments. If you plan to use a combination of motifs, you will need to use the lines to check and help the spacing and balance.

QUANTITY OF QUILTING IN BORDERS

It is advisable to plan to quilt borders in a similar proportion to the amount of quilting in the centre section. If a closely quilted border surrounds a centre which has only minimal outline quilting, the quilt will neither look 'right' nor lie flat. The reverse also applies.

One tried and tested idea for quilting borders is to use a scaled-down version of one of the main quilting patterns or motifs. You can see how this works on the quilt on page 94. If you double the number of main lines on such a scaled-down pattern, the smaller pattern will look subtly different to the original.

If you have a deep border surrounding pieced or appliqué blocks, you could fill it with simple crosshatching to give plenty of texture and enrichment without detracting from the centre of the quilt. Many Amish quilts have one or more borders quilted in this way and the crosshatching contrasts well with the other quilting patterns used. One student who professed not to like quilting was persuaded to use crosshatching on the border of her first quilt as a means of finishing it quickly without too much quilting. Not only does the crosshatching look good, but she also found it much easier to work than outline quilting with all its negotiation of seam allowances – her views on quilting have been somewhat modified as a result and her quilt is beautiful.

BACKGROUNDS

Once all major elements of the design have been chosen, it is all too easy to gloss over the question of background quilting. The balance and contrast from background quilting can greatly enhance the main design(s). Too little background quilting (it is almost impossible to have too much!) or a background of inappropriate proportion can detract from an otherwise excellent design. Closely worked backgrounds give prominence to the main pattern by 'holding down' the subsidiary areas, thus allowing the larger unquilted (negative) spaces of the main pattern to become more prominent.

Many quilters groan at the prospect of 'all that stitching' when close background quilting is suggested. They need a little persuasion to see that the quantity of quilting needed for a close textured effect is also a highly efficient way of becoming a quality quilter. If practice

Detail showing a crosshatched or grid border on a quilt made by Helen Whittingham

makes perfect, then background quilting is the ideal vehicle to improve individual stitching technique and acquire that rhythm.

DOUBLE-LINE PATTERNS

Double lines frequently show to excellent advantage in background quilting. They give the impression of complexity without taxing your abilities. Closely spaced double lines also define the main pattern well. A cursory glance at old quilts shows how well the function and effectiveness of a double line of stitching was understood. Some long-suffering students have suggested that my epitaph will need to be carved in double lines before my spirit will finally rest!

Where a straightforward crosshatch or waffle background (Fig 22k, page 45) seems almost, but not quite right, doubling the lines (Fig 22l, page 45) can look better. Parallel lines assume more interest when doubled and repay far more in impact than the effort of quilting them.

STIPPLING

The ultimate background quilting technique is stippling. This labour-intensive method is superbly dramatic in its effect. Because the randomly placed stitches are so closely

Fig 28a

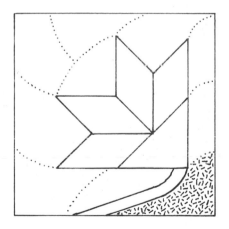

Fig 28b

Samples showing closely worked background quilting

packed together, any adjacent unquilted areas are thrown into much sharper relief. Stippling is frequently found on old masterpiece quilts, and often accompanied by trapunto work on the main pattern, which defines and enhances the texture even more.

There is no one correct way to stipple. The stitches are closely worked in seemingly random fashion. For your first stippling experiment, choose a very small background area – perhaps the centre of a feathered wreath or the space around a pieced tulip. Then rather than tackling this small area as a whole, work one tiny sub-section at a time, making no more than two stitches at a time before changing direction (Figs 28a and b, page 57).

ECHO QUILTING

Echo quilting is exactly what is says – the quilting lines echo the main pattern outlines, whether they are pieced, appliquéd or quilted. As a specific technique, echo

Detail of Apricot Twist quilt designed and made by Jennie Langmead showing close background quilting and stippling worked in the centre of the star motif

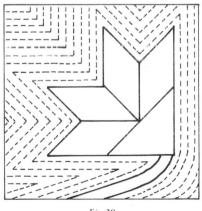

Fig 29

quilting was developed to greatest effect within the Hawaiian tradition (see page 60).

The strong fluid lines of background echo quilting (Fig 29) reinforce the bold appearance of appliqué shapes. Spacing between the lines of quilting is generally judged by eye (or width of thumb) rather than painstaking and accurate measurement. Echo quilting can give interest to the spaces between patterns and change the emphasis of that space. Worked at ¼ inch (0.6 cm) intervals it can give a close-textured background without the intensity of stippling or meandering.

MEANDER QUILTING

Meander quilting (Fig 30) is often seen in machine-quilted pieces but can also be done by hand. The quilted lines meander almost aimlessly over the background area producing texture without specific pattern and giving unobtrusive background quilting without measuring or marking. A formal type of meander quilting (Fig 31) can

Fig 30

be seen on some waistcoats and petticoats from the eighteenth century.

Fig 31

CORDED QUILTING

Corded quilting combines very well with meandering – the cording gives smooth lines in high relief which contrast well with the tighter scale of the meandering lines. You might like to try a small piece of flat (unpadded) quilting using meandering for the background and cording for the main patterns. Instead of using running stitch, experiment with backstitch, which gives a continuous rather than a broken line and enhances the finished effect.

If you find it difficult to select just the right background for a design, why not sidetrack your decision and begin

The three Hawaiian appliqué pieces (above left) are examples of echo quilting. Used in the curved centre section between the feathers (above), echo quilting can give interest to the spaces between pattern motifs

Fig 32

a practice piece as shown in Fig 32? Tack (baste) a 24-inch (60-cm) square with wadding (batting) and backing and try out various backgrounds, such as closely spaced parallel lines, waffle quilting, diamonds, and so on. You could also use this practice piece to try freehand pattern marking. Work on this sampler before you stitch more important projects in much the same way as you would run through a few scales before embarking on a concert performance.

PROJECT: OHIO STAR SMALL QUILT OR CUSHION

Why not practise some of the ideas in this chapter on a small quilt? The finished quilt measures 34×47 inches (86.3×119.3 cm).

TECHNIQUES USED

Tacking
Outline quilting
Background quilting
Freehand marking
Using masking tape to mark straight lines

YOU WILL NEED

½ yd. (0.5 m) each of 3 fabrics (2 complementary, 1 contrasting)
⅔ yd. (0.67 m) fabric for sashing
1 yd. (1 m) fabric for borders

2 oz. wadding (batting) to measure 36×49 in. (90×122.5 cm)
1½ yds. backing fabric (cut and seamed if necessary) to measure 36×49 in. (90×122.5 cm)
Matching threads
Pins
Card or plastic for templates
Fabric marker
Frame or hoop
Masking tape
Betweens needles of your choice

METHOD

1 Make templates A and B (Figs 33a and b). For handpiecing trace the inner solid line, for machine piecing use the outer dotted line.

2 Mark around the templates on the wrong side of the fabric.
Note: If you are handpiecing, mark the solid line on your fabric. This will be the sewing line. When you cut around it, leave a generous seam allowance. For machine

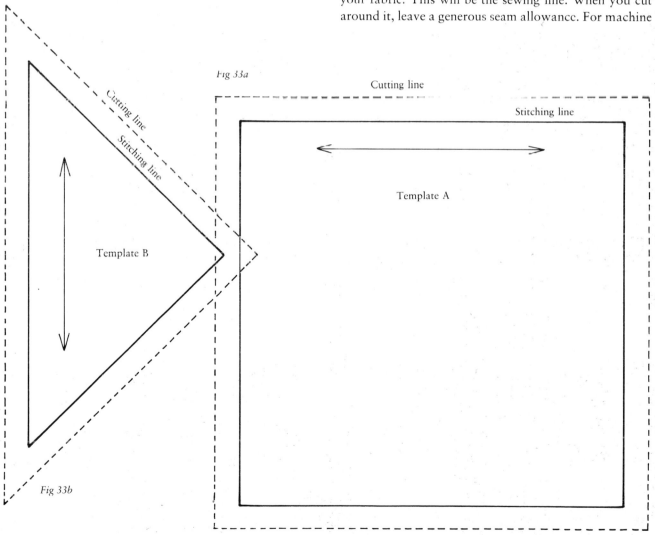

Fig 33a

Cutting line

Stitching line

Template A

Cutting line

Stitching line

Template B

Fig 33b

piecing you need to mark the dotted cutting line only – you will then align the raw edges and stitch with a consistent seam allowance, using the machine presser foot as a guide. Be sure to match the arrows to the straight grain of the fabric.

3 Mark and cut out

    4 of square B from background fabric

    1 of square B from main fabric

    8 of triangle A from background fabric

    8 of triangle A from main fabric.

Fig 33c shows how each block will look.

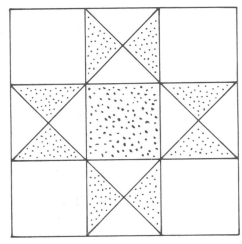

Fig 33c

4 With wrong sides together, seam one dark triangle A to one light triangle A as shown in Fig 34.

Fig 34

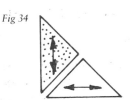

For hand piecing, stitch only on the marked lines (Fig 35a). If you are machine piecing, stitch right from one edge to the other (Fig 35b).

Fig 35a   *Fig 35b*

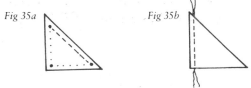

Repeat until you have joined together 8 dark/light triangle units.

5 Press all seams to one side. Press towards the darker fabric to avoid shadowing through.

6 Join pairs of triangle units together to form squares as shown in Fig 36 and press again.

Fig 36

7 Now the pieced squares can be joined to the cut squares to form strips as shown in Fig 37.

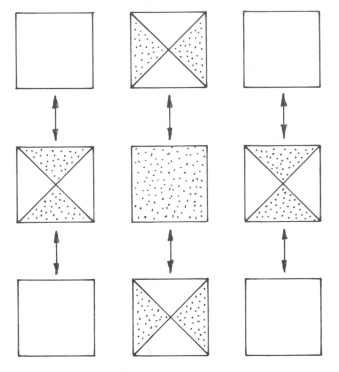

Fig 37

Press again and join the three strips together to complete the block. Press the completed block on the wrong side first and then the right side.

8 Make a total of 6 Ohio Star blocks.

9 Cut strips 1½ in. (3.8 cm) wide from the sashing fabric and strips 4½ in. (11.3 cm) wide from the border fabric.

10 Join the blocks with sashing strips as shown in Fig 38a and add borders as in Fig 38b.

11 Lay out backing, wadding and pieced top and tack together (see pages 28-29).

12 Look again at the photograph of the quilt. You need to decide whether you want each block to be quilted identically or differently.

13 With the quilt sandwich in a frame or under some tension, mark your chosen designs onto the pieced top. If you already have some templates or stencils that you would like to try, mark around these in the chosen

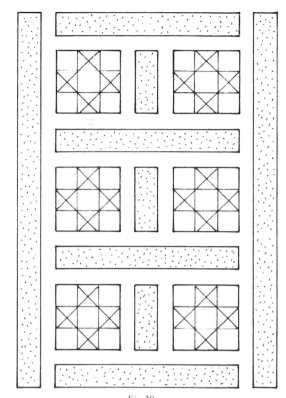

Fig 38a

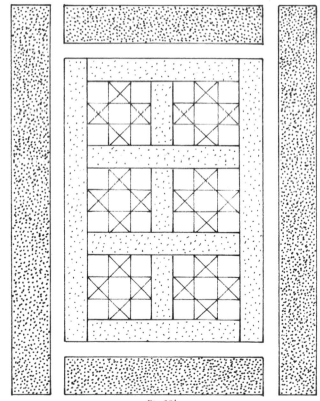

Fig 38b

14 Outline quilt the main star shape of each block, stitching ¼ in. (0.6 cm) away from the seams. Alternatively, quilt 'in the ditch', that is very close to, or actually on the seams. Figs 39a, b and c show some quilting patterns for you to consider.

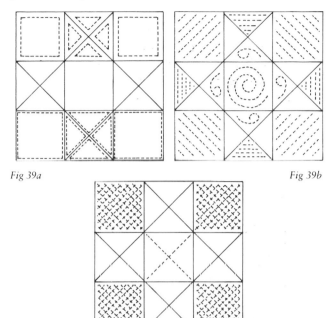

Fig 39a   *Fig 39b*

Fig 39c

15 Work systematically out from the centre of the quilt or across from one corner (see page 35). You now have seam allowances to negotiate – a little care and patience with these will be well rewarded.

16 Quilt all around the inside of the border.

17 Remove all tacking threads.

18 Making a small quilt not only gives you an opportunity to experiment with marking up and quilting, but is a manageable size for trying out one of the finishing techniques described in Chapter Three. Good luck! You will find instructions and suggestions for labelling your quilt in Chapter Nine.

If you like, make just one block and follow the sequence shown in Fig 40 to add border strips to make a cushion.

Fig 40

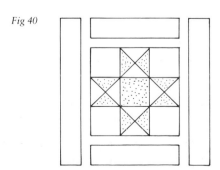

position. Otherwise, practise freehand drawing for curving lines (or use a flexicurve as a guide) or use masking tape for straight lines.

Chapter Five

DIFFERENT TYPES OF QUILTING

HAND-SEWN TECHNIQUES

*A*ll of the hand-stitched techniques described here can be used successfully either singly or in combination.

TRAPUNTO

Masterpiece quilts were often enhanced by additional stuffing or padding which brought selected areas of the main design into higher relief. Known as trapunto, this technique is becoming increasingly popular again.

The additional stuffing of the stitched shapes can be done before or after other quilting. If you make it the first stage, stitch the outlines of the shapes through the top fabric and a very lightweight second fabric such as cheesecloth or mull which has a loose, open weave through which to push small pieces of stuffing. Many instructions for trapunto quilting recommend drawing the design on the lightweight fabric and stitching from the under side, but your stitches may look better worked from the top side. The stitches should be fairly close and as even as possible. If you work from the top, your pattern markings should be easily removable. (See Chapter Two for detailed discussion of marking methods.) One advantage of working from the top is that you are not restricted to running stitch – stem, chain or backstitch can all look effective. A contrasting thread can give even greater emphasis. Once the stitched outlines are complete, extra stuffing can be inserted, a little at a time, until the desired effect is achieved. Be cautious! This process is very easy to overdo. Overstuffing results in distortions of the top fabric which mar the final effect. You can use a variety of implements – toothpicks, cocktail sticks, crochet hooks, tapestry needles – to push the wadding through the back fabric. Either push the threads apart, or carefully make a small slit in the back fabric (Fig 41). Use tiny pieces of stuffing one at a time, and push them gently up to the stitched lines (Fig 42). Slits should be secured with a neat herringbone stitch (Fig 43).

When stuffing large areas it may be simpler to work through several small slits at the back rather than filling the space through one larger opening.

If you plan to use trapunto techniques on a piece which has a layer of wadding (batting), work the trapunto

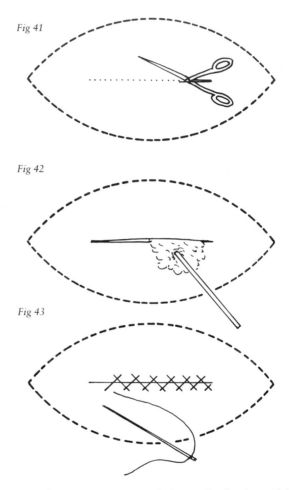

Fig 41

Fig 42

Fig 43

sections first, using a very lightweight backing fabric which can be trimmed away before adding the wadding and backing. Work subsequent quilting lines as close as possible to the stuffed areas to secure them.

American quilter Sue Rodgers advocates using a long fine weaver's needle threaded with soft yarn when working trapunto in conjunction with wadded quilting. The trapunto areas are worked after the plain wadded quilting is finished. The needle is inserted through the backing layer of the quilt and the shape filled with the yarn. After the yarn has been clipped very close to the surface, the small puncture holes in the backing fabric can be eased back into position leaving little trace. There is

These satin cushions and bags have been worked in corded quilting in styles and colours that are typical of the 1930s and 40s. (Courtesy of Marianne Grime)

no need to slit the fabric and the puncture holes are insignificant if you do not tug too hard as the yarn is pulled through. Subsequent laundering and handling of the finished piece also helps to settle the fabric threads back into position.

CORDED OR ITALIAN QUILTING

In this technique lengths of yarn or strands of soft wool are threaded from the reverse of the work through channels formed by lines of stitching to give a raised or corded effect. Corded quilting, particularly popular in the 1930s and 40s, is very simple and satisfying to do. Many standard quilting and embroidery patterns adapt very well; convert the main pattern outlines into double lines which will form stitched channels for the cording (Fig 44).

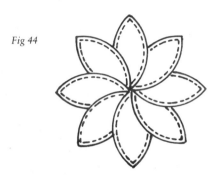

Fig 44

A lightweight openweave fabric is tacked (basted) to the reverse side of the top fabric and the parallel lines which form the channel for the cord are worked in running, back, chain or stem stitch. Contrasting thread can be used, and the stitching can be worked from either the top or reverse side. The channels can be stitched by machine, but do not overshoot at the point where lines intersect. A twin-needle machine can make very short work of the entire process, but do pay attention to those intersections!

After stitching the design (Fig 45), thread a tapestry needle with soft wool, cord or coloured yarn. Working from the wrong side, use the blunt end of the needle to push the threads of the backing fabric apart and slide the needle a little way along the stitched channel; (Fig 46). Bring the needle out again through the backing fabric and pull gently to ensure that the yarn lies smoothly. Re-insert the needle at this same exit point to continue cording, but do not pull the yarn completely through. Leave a small loop of yarn each time you re-insert the needle (Fig 47) so the cording fits well and smoothly around curves and angles. If you need to work around a sharp angle or corner, bring the needle out exactly on the point of the angle, leave a loop, re-insert the needle at the same point and continue cording in the new direction.

When you have finished cording, make a few small cross-stitches to anchor the tails of cord in place (Fig 48).

You can use the simple quilting pattern given on page 42 to practise both cording and stuffing techniques. Note that where pairs of lines meet and cross, one channel should remain open.

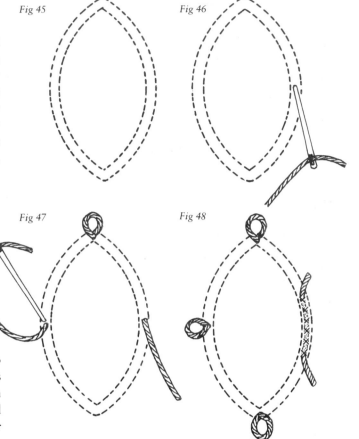

Fig 45

Fig 46

Fig 47

Fig 48

SHADOW QUILTING

In shadow quilting, as distinct from shadow appliqué, coloured yarns or threads are inserted between stitched lines to produce subtly coloured shapes.

Shadow quilting is a development of trapunto and follows the same general steps. Strongly coloured sewing thread for the outline stitching is a positive advantage here and any thin top fabric, organza, lawn or lightweight cotton, may be used. The ends of the cording need to be folded back and stitched in place to avoid being visible from the right side. Choose bright threads and yarns as the final result will be considerably muted, depending on the thickness of the top fabric.

FLAT QUILTING

Quilting without any wadding (batting), as you might expect, is known as flat quilting. It was often used for summer covers where warmth was a minor consideration.

This is quilting at its simplest and most basic. Two

Quilted 'landscapes'

layers of fabric are stitched together, usually with running stitch, sometimes with back or chain stitch. There is no layer of wadding between the two fabrics. This type of quilting was often used to finish patchworks composed of many small pieces such as hexagons or diamonds where the large number of seam allowances would have made wadded quilting difficult.

SASHIKO QUILTING

The traditional Japanese flat quilting technique, known as sashiko, has become increasingly popular and offers much scope for today's quilter in both design and application. Its origins lie in lines of running stitch worked in coarse thread on working garments. This additional stitching gave prolonged wear to clothes in the way that leather or suede elbow patches extend the life of sweaters and jackets.

Many linear patterns were subsequently adapted to the sashiko technique to great decorative effect. Sashiko can help develop even stitching, and many of its traditional patterns can be successfully adapted as background patterns in wadded quilting.

True sashiko is running stitch worked through two layers of fabric, traditionally indigo-dyed, using a coarse thread of contrasting colour, usually white. Contemporary sashiko demands only a strong colour contrast. Suitable threads include coton à broder or cotton perlé #5 or #8. Use a sharps needle with an eye large enough to accommodate the thicker thread.

Tack (baste) rather than pin the two layers of fabric together and begin with a knot which can either be hidden between the two layers of fabric or left at the back of the work. Secure completed lines of stitching by weaving back along three or four stitches on the reverse side, or weave the needle between the stitched fabric layers to finish off invisibly. Starting and finishing threads can alternatively be left as loose lengths at the edges of the work and knotted to form mock tassels after the stitching has been completed.

MACHINE QUILTING

Machine quilting has had an undeservedly bad press for a number of years and for far too long has been considered inferior to 'real' – i.e. hand – quilting. The reason remains a mystery, since wonderful effects can be achieved with machine quilting. Perhaps the relative speed of the technique irked committed hand quilters; perhaps some of the first machine-quilted pieces seen in exhibitions did not display the much-coveted soft texture of hand work.

Machine quilting, when thoughtfully done, looks superb and equally as good as its counterpart. Hand quilting also looks superb if thoughtfully done – it is just different. A machine-quilted line is well defined with a crisp furrow created by the line of stitching. Hand quilting forms a broken line and a softer furrow. Machine quilting is becoming more sophisticated by the day, and some of the results are truly lovely. If you would like to try machine quilting but have an uneasy feeling that it is 'not allowed', remember that sewing machines have been used since the 1860s. Machine quilting (often very neatly done) is found on many quilts after this time. One of the most succinct appraisals of machine quilting comes from Harriet Hargrave, American quilter and teacher, who reminds us that this technique should be regarded as hand quilting with an electric needle.

PREPARATION FOR MACHINE QUILTING

Good machine quilting requires similar attitudes and practice to hand quilting. In other words, start with modest, realistic expectations and be prepared to learn as you go.

Pinning To prepare a quilt for machine quilting requires the same careful centring of the three layers as hand quilting (see page 28). Tacking (basting) is replaced by safety pins positioned evenly from the centre. The layers should be smoothed out as the pins are secured. Thick wadding (batting) will need to be pinned at 2 to 3 inch (5 to 7.5 cm) intervals, thinner wadding can be pinned at 3 to 4 inch (7.5 to 10 cm) intervals. Use safety pins in preference to tacking or straight pins; they will not move while the quilt is being manoeuvred during the quilting process. Straight pins can stab your hands, and tacking stitches have an annoying habit of getting tangled around the presser foot.

Folding Attention to pinning and smoothing, together with planned folding of the quilt layers, can make machine quilting much easier. The folding is needed to avoid manhandling endless layers into position once

A selection of sashiko quilting worked by students in traditional colours

Quilting a brightly coloured nursery quilt by machine. Notice the quilter's comfortable supporting chair. The quilt is rolled up to make it easier to handle while working

machining has begun. Harriet Hargrave recommends folding the left side of the quilt towards the centre and tightly rolling the right side of the quilt, also towards the centre. The rolled section can be secured with several bicycle clips – another shining example of quilters inventiveness! Correctly done, this should leave 4 to 6 inches (10 to 15 cm) of the quilt exposed, ready to go under the needle. The rolled and folded quilt can now be accordion-folded from one end, again working towards the centre and then on to the far edge.

Organising space Once you have prepared the quilt layers, you need to prepare your sewing machine and the space you will be working in. Handling quilt layers is much easier if there is an adequate work surface at the back and left side of the machine. It is even better if these surfaces are level with the bed of the machine, but this may require ingenuity and some do-it-yourself skills. Machine quilting supremo Harriet Hargrave offers some ideas in *Heirloom Machine Quilting* if you would like to pursue this.

Machine quilting, unlike hand quilting, cannot be quickly picked up and put down again. Concentration is usually more intense and work periods generally last longer. Sit on a supportive chair adjusted to a comfortable height, and move as many lamps as necessary to provide a good bright light directly on the working area.

Preparing the machine Check that the machine is clean, oiled and in good general running order and remove the piled-up lint that lurks under every bobbin case. Refer to the owner's manual and check both the top and bobbin tensions. Work several lines of stitching using two layers of scrap cloth and one of wadding to see if either tension needs to be adjusted.

Additions to the machine It is possible to buy a walking foot for most sewing machines. If it fits well, this can make any machine quilting based on straight lines much easier, since the quilt layers can be stitched and moved evenly without too many tucks and pleats appearing in the backing fabric.

If you decide to branch out into more complex machine quilting designs, you will need a darning foot to practise 'fancy' quilting designs. A quilting foot is usually an embroidery foot with a gauge bar at the back which helps you to work evenly spaced lines.

Threads A fine good-quality invisible nylon thread used with a fine cotton thread in the bobbin produces an almost hand-quilted effect. The transparency and fineness of the nylon thread make it nearly invisible on the quilt top, so the quilted texture is seen before the actual lines of machine stitching. There is also an excellent ever-expanding choice of machine embroidery threads, including metallic and shaded, for you to experiment with.

BEGINNING TO QUILT

'In the ditch' If you are just beginning, this is one of the easiest machine techniques. Of course, there must be seams in the top layer to quilt alongside – it is best to start your machine quilting career on a spare patchwork block. (If you do not have any patchwork to practise on, try quilting grid or crosshatch lines on plain fabric as described below.)

Try out several rows of stitches first on a sample. Layer the same top, wadding (batting) and backing fabrics as those used for the piece you want to quilt. Do a test run to see if any final adjustments of tension or stitch length need to be made. Remembering to test before starting each project is a Good Quilting Habit, just like remembering to test fabric markers for ease of removal.

'In the ditch' means quilting either exactly on the seam itself or fractionally to one side of it. Working at the side of the seam is easy if you know that the seam allowances have been pressed to one side. Quilt on the side that has no seam allowance underneath as close to the seam as you can. Quilting exactly on the seam works best when the seam allowances have been pressed open.

Allover grids can be worked over large areas and are the equivalent of large-scale crosshatching. Stitch one of the centre lines first and continue working towards the edges in the sequence shown (Fig 49). Return to the central diagonal line and complete the second half. Repeat the sequence to complete the crossing lines (Fig 50).

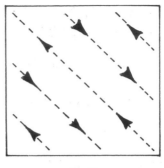

Fig 49

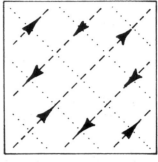

Fig 50

Quilting curved and complex designs Make a sample for your first attempts. Use a darning foot and either drop or cover the feed dogs – consult your manual for how to do this. You will be in control of the stitch length, which will vary depending on the speed of the machine and how quickly you move the fabric under the darning foot.

Begin by bringing the bobbin thread up to the quilt surface – this prevents it from jamming underneath. Hold both threads at the back or side of the foot until the first few stitches are made; it is advisable then to pause and clip both threads. Maintain as even and consistent a speed as possible while moving the layers around under the darning foot. Don't push and pull but keep the 'sandwich' moving smoothly. As you become more accustomed to the feel of this process, try 'drawing' curved shapes. With practice, you should feel confident enough to tackle something larger than test pieces.

When starting and finishing threads, do not backstitch. You will only jam the threads and fabric into an ugly mess. Start with the shortest possible stitch length and then increase the setting to the required length. Decrease the stitch length back to the shortest setting to finish off. Tiny stitches, which are almost impossible to unpick, should not unravel. If you feel uncomfortable doing this, just start and stop without any adjustment of the stitch length. Whichever method you choose, take the top thread through to the back and tie both threads together in a knot. Thread both ends through a needle and sink both threads and knot through the quilt backing and into the wadding.

PROJECT: TRAPUNTO AND CORDED CUSHION COVER

Practise these techniques using the 'Tudor Rose' design on page 42.

YOU WILL NEED

½ yd. (0.5 m) top fabric
¼ yd. (0.25 m) cheesecloth, mull or other openweave fabric (this is your 'second' fabric)
Soft yarn for cording (usually sold by the hank)
Large tapestry needle
Synthetic wadding (batting) snipped into tiny pieces
Thread to match or tone with top fabric
Fabric marker (test for removal if you will be using it on the top fabric)

1 Trace and complete the design (Fig 20) given on page 42 on to the lightweight second fabric, or mark the completed design on the top fabric.

2 Centre and tack (baste) the top and second fabrics together.

3 Work even running stitches on all the marked lines. Starting and finishing threads may be left on the second fabric. If you have chosen to work from the top, other stitches such as backstitch, chainstitch or stem stitch may be used.

4 When all the lines have been stitched, thread soft yarn through the channels. Work through the second fabric on the reverse side using a tapestry needle. Leave loops of yarn at intervals, especially at sharp points, steep curves and intersections. This cording stage should seem speedy – and almost magical in terms of instant results!

5 With the cording completed, begin work on the trapunto areas. Either cut the second fabric or push apart the threads so that tiny scraps of wadding (batting) can be inserted one at a time. Push the wadding close up against the stitched lines, but don't cram too much into each space. Check the front of the work frequently to see the effect and when to stop. Fill all the trapunto areas in this way.

6 After the trapunto areas have all been filled, close any slits in the second fabric with herringbone stitch to keep the wadding in place.

7 Take a few moments to admire your work before making it into a cushion cover using your preferred method.

Fig 51b

Fig 51c

PROJECT: MACHINE-QUILTED TABLE RUNNER

Measurements: 51×17 inches (127.5×42.5 cm)

YOU WILL NEED

Scraps for 3×12 in. (30 cm) patchwork blocks

1 yd. (1 m) backing fabric

⅔ yd. (0.67 m) fabric for 'filler' triangles or 4 triangles of fabric cut 12½×17½ in. (31.3×43.8 cm)

2 oz. wadding (batting) to measure 53×19 in. (132.5×47.5 cm)

Fine thread for machine quilting

1 Using the patterns printed on page 63, Figs 33a and b, make templates A and B for an Ohio Star block, or use other block patterns of your choice as we have done for the photograph below.

2 Mark and cut out the requisite number of pieces from your chosen fabrics and seam together in the sequence described and shown in Figs 34–37 on page 64 to make three blocks in total.

3 Join the three blocks together with the 'filler' triangles into a strip. You may prefer to add the binding now.

4 Measure and cut wadding (batting) and backing so that both are larger than the finished top.

5 Carefully pin-baste the three layers together as described on page 71.

6 Machine quilt around the main shapes of each star and elsewhere as desired.

7 Secure all starting and finishing threads, and complete binding. Remember to label your work.

Chapter Six

DESIGN SOURCES AND PRINCIPLES

*Q*uilting patterns come from many sources, especially the host of publications for quilters worldwide. Specialist magazines print quilting patterns of various sizes and styles; many collections are available in books and as packets and stencils which give a variety of patterns for quilting and suggestions about using and rearranging them.

You may feel that you would like to try something just a little more individual but are not sure where or how to begin. If you have arrived at quilting via patchwork and appliqué, riffle through your template collection for inspiration. Many shapes can be used to construct simple quilting patterns, as shown in Figs 53a, b, c, d and e, and lots of appliqué patterns can be adapted in full or in part

for quilting. Look at embroidery patterns, too. The Jacobean-style patterns in Fig 54 would adapt well for quilting with only a little simplification. For just the right quilting motif to use on a pieced or appliqué top, perhaps you could adapt and develop the pattern you have already worked. The following suggestions for pattern sources and their development, together with repetition, contrast and variety of scale can be applied equally to all quilting techniques.

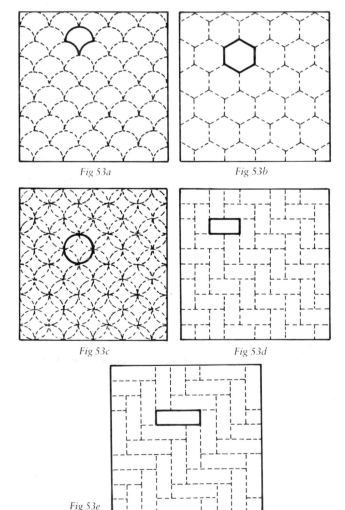

Fig 53a

Fig 53b

Fig 53c

Fig 53d

Fig 53e

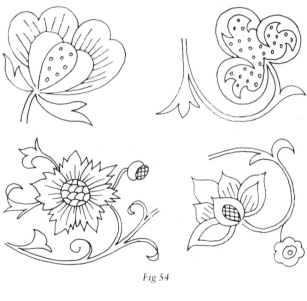

Fig 54

Patterns and motifs which recur within any quilting tradition are those which have wide appeal and versatility. For instance, feathered shapes and patterns based on circles are frequently found on quilts and quilted garments of any era. One obvious source of patterns for quilting is old quilts (see page 136). If you find the design of an old quilt particularly pleasing, use it, but do credit the work as a 'remake'. You may want to base your own design on an existing quilt, with a few changes to make it more individual – this is how the tradition moves on, and you will certainly increase your appreciation of other quilters' work.

There is also a great variety of patterns from other sources. Why not look further afield for design inspiration? Design sources abound; look at printed patterns, wrought ironwork, woodcarving, ceramics, wallpaper, textiles and architectural detail. Patterns such as feathers,

A carpet design was the source for this quilt in progress

leaves, fans and shells which have stood the test of time (Fig 55) tend to have clean, simple and flowing lines. Quilters have always created and adapted patterns from everyday objects; plates, saucers and cups were used as templates for circular patterns, and the designs on them could also be adapted.

A treasure trove of designs can be found in books on the decorative arts. Their illustrations and line drawings from many areas of decorative design – carvings, textiles, ceramics, metalwork, etc. – place a whole world of ideas in your hands.

Seeing a design and recognising its possibilities is easy,

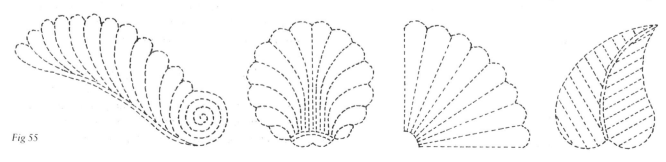

Fig 55

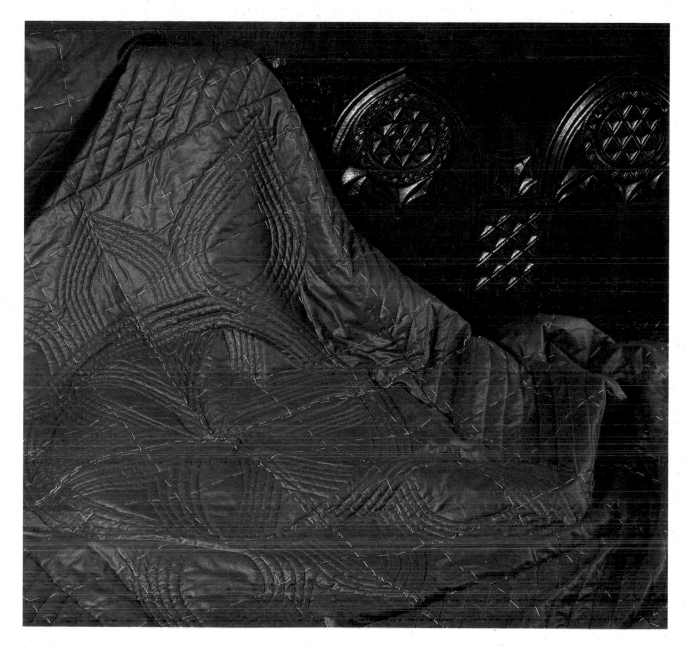

A quilt in progress, developed by Margaret Salt from an old carved wooden chest

but how do you progress from looking at, say, the piece of wrought ironwork shown here to using it as a quilting pattern?

The first step is to make a sketch of the main shapes by focusing only on the outlines. One virtually foolproof way is to project 35 mm slides onto a sheet of paper taped to the wall. Draw around the outlines, varying the size of the image by moving the projector closer or further away. Some detail can be added using the original as a guide, but be selective – you do not have to reproduce all the lines.

The patterns on wrought ironwork (top) and ceramic tiles (bottom left) could inspire many ideas for quilting, and the motif from a carved chair (bottom right) could easily be adapted

Remember also that sections of the pattern can be isolated and re-grouped to make a new design.

Ceramic tile patterns such as the ones shown here can be simplified and perhaps re-sized to furnish handsome designs for quilted cushions or blocks in a pieced quilt.

Marquetry and inlay patterns have many applications for needlework generally and even the simplest wood-carvings offer unexpectedly rich pickings. One quilter spotted an old carved wooden chest and managed to take a rubbing from it. By varying the scale of just one pattern and adding a simple crosshatch background, she was able to plan the sumptuous quilt shown here.

Another quilter jotted down some patterns from a piece of medieval silverwork. The sketches remained in her notebook for some time, but three of the motifs were eventually developed into the quilt shown here. She repeated the two main motifs with variations in scale and careful attention to contrast and balance. The use of crosshatching has been very successful in this quilt; the straight lines contrast with the open curving lines of the

main patterns as well as framing the design areas. The closeness of the crosshatching gives a pleasing change in proportion to the wider spacing of the main pattern lines and the overall simplicity is most appealing. Look at the sketches of the motifs in Figs 56a, b and c and imagine how you would group them. You might develop the same

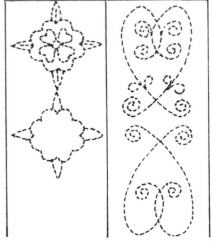

Fig 57

motifs into a strippy design (Fig 57), or re-arrange them on a smaller scale for a cushion cover.

A visit to your local museum could present you with more ideas than you could ever use if you go with an open mind and an open notebook! Everyday cups and saucers can suggest pattern ideas – the tulip on a favourite Susie Cooper teacup (Fig 58) has distinct promise! A variety of

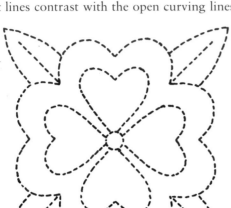

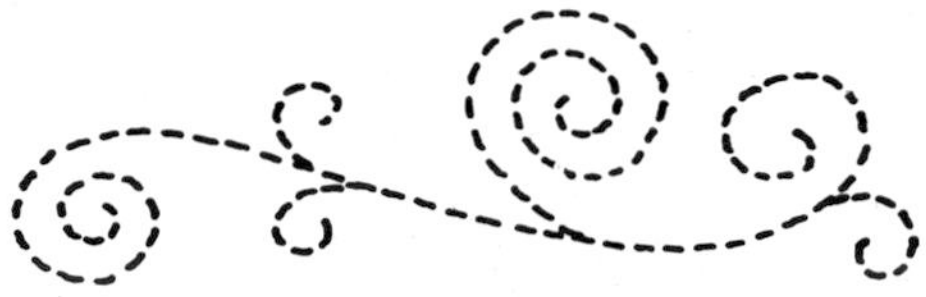

Fig 56a

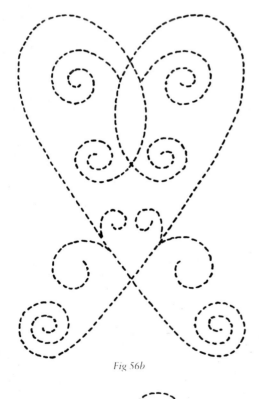

Fig 56b

Fig 58

arrangements can be made quite easily by simplifying and altering a basic tulip shape as in Fig 59, page 84.

Try linking the motifs in these sketches in your own way, changing and adapting lines as necessary.

Motifs used on packaging, textiles, wallpapers will also give you food for thought. Be open to possibilities –

Fig 56c

Prize-winning quilt designed and made by Ilse Oldfield, its design based on a medieval silverwork pattern

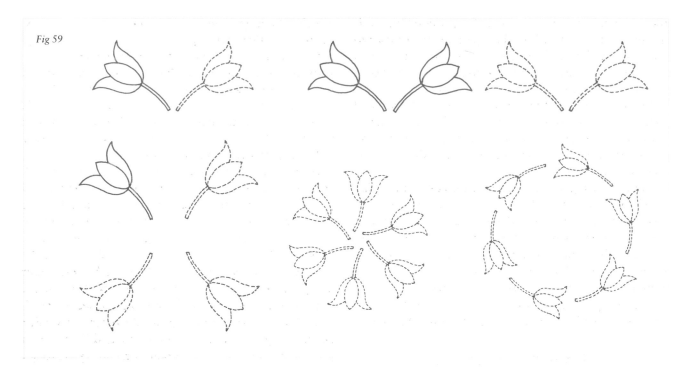

Fig 59

inspiration is everywhere. Quilters, practised in 'mental jogging', have been found gazing intently at cracked ice patterns on frozen puddles and even the whorls of their own fingerprints! Soon you will be able to 'find' a quilting pattern in almost everything you see. (You may think this is exhilarating and exciting – others may not!) Remember as you look around that strong fluid lines show better than short intricate ones. The basic lines of any pattern may be easier to see if you half-close your eyes in the same way that you might resolve dark, medium and light tones of fabric for patchwork.

When sketching pattern ideas from any source, you may find it helpful to use a pad of squared paper. Sketches and doodles on squared paper can easily be enlarged or reduced by photocopier or by the square for square method (Figs 60a and b), and the lines may be helpful to you when jotting down designs.

Always keep a small notebook handy – it will be less cumbersome than a camera and can be used anywhere (many museums forbid photography) – or note down ideas when you are back home. It doesn't matter if your sketches are not faithful replicas – recording in this way is a Good Habit to develop and great for improving hand/ eye co-ordination. Of course, we all mean to record as we go; few of us actually do, but persevere – you will find your speed and ability to put ideas onto paper improves rapidly.

Once you have begun to 'see' quilting patterns everywhere, you are well on the way to being able to design for yourself. Many students find it quite easy to jot down patterns from a wide variety of sources and even devise

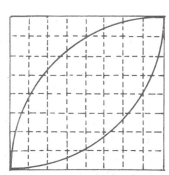

Fig 60a

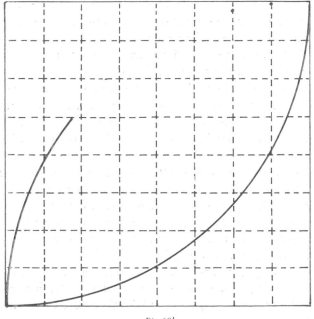

Fig 60b

84

their own patterns from pencil and paper doodlings; it is not so easy to visualise how these patterns can be used to make a complete quilting design. Certain patterns will almost dictate their own terms as to the way they should be arranged; others are not so compliant.

The first consideration for quilt design is the size and shape of the planned project; choice and arrangement of pattern within this area is the next step. If there is no organisation of the individual patterns, the result is confused and chaotic.

The main categories or styles of wholecloth quilt design which provide a basic framework for pattern arrangement are medallion, where there is a centre, corners and borders; strippy, where patterns run in unbroken lines; allover, where the patterns cover the entire surface without a particular plan; and asymmetrical, where the patterns are deliberately arranged so that they do not repeat in a predictable rhythmic fashion. Of these four styles, the most familiar are the medallion and the strippy.

GOOD DESIGN

What is good design? How does it apply to quilts and why? Can you compose a good design without intensive art school study? Does design really matter? The answer to the last two questions is a resounding 'Yes'— good design does matter, and you can create good designs without formal art training.

In her seminal pamphlet 'White on White' Jean Dubois wrote: 'Part of good design is taste . . . but there are rules that we can ignore only at our peril. One is the rule of contrast; one is the rule of repetition; one is the rule of balance.' In other words, *good design has a main theme and balance.* These principles – simplicity, balance, contrast, scale and repetition – are also basic to many other disciplines. Simple designs are often the most effective; it is not essential to use many different motifs in order to create elaborate designs.

Simplicity means what it says – there is no need to use many different patterns. Instead, look for just two or three patterns as a beginning. *Balance* refers to the placement of pattern, which should not be unduly 'busy' or crowded at any one point of the design. *Contrast* allows the main patterns to be seen easily; for example, curved line patterns often show better against a background of straight lines. *Scale* is the use of patterns of appropriate size and also the varying of size of specific patterns. *Repetition* of one or more patterns within a design gives a sense of order and continuity.

By keeping things simple and not filling all available space you provide resting space for the eye. Look at the quilts shown on pages 83 and 93. One reason the main patterns are so well-defined is that the borders of

crosshatching give texture but do not compete for attention in their own right.

Good quilt design sometimes defies detailed analysis. Ultimately the design should look pleasing and complete. It has perhaps more to do with economy of line, and what you leave out may be more important than what is included. A design based on two or three patterns with variation of scale may look much better than many different patterns crowded together.

Drawing and design for quilting is just having enough confidence to use pencil and paper to show main areas of pattern. 'Design' can baffle and intimidate and the term itself strikes terror into many hearts; the instinctive response is 'I can't draw'. Design is *not* the same as drawing. Design is the planning, while drawing is the making of lines on paper. Jean Dubois defined the quilt design process superbly as 'simply a series of decisions'.

Anyone can make good designs without highly developed drawing skills. Just to prove the point, try a quick pencil and paper exercise. See how many different ways you can arrange hearts of various scale using the rough sketches in Fig 61 to help you.

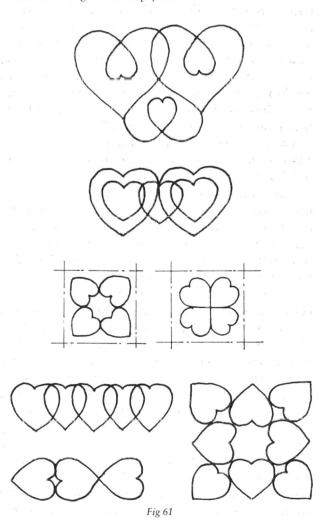

Fig 61

GROUPING PATTERNS

Once you have decided on your overall design plan, experiment with different pattern groupings. Your quilt design does not have to be an original work of art with every line of your own devising. There are so many patterns, both traditional and contemporary, that you will probably be spoilt for choice. Try arranging some of the patterns shown in Fig 55 on page 79 and see what combinations you can make.

Medallion patterns are combined to make a central design which usually dominates the total quilt area, either by the scale of patterns and/or the size of the total medallion itself. Complementing and contrasting borders and corners are added to frame the important central area. Spaces not filled by medallion, corner or border patterns may have contrasting background quilting. Look quickly at the quilt shown above.

A wholecloth medallion quilt

First impressions show a very ornate and, at first sight, highly complex, medallion quilt. Now study the skeleton of the design in Fig 62, above right.

Working out from the centre, there is a rose with concentric circles, then a variation of the shell pattern (sometimes referred to as 'hairbrush'). This shell or hairbrush is arranged around the central rose to form a larger circular design. From here pairs of pierced feathers extend the central medallion area. Notice how these three patterns relate to each other: they are all curved-edge patterns which contrast well with the large area of waffle or crosshatched background quilting. The rose pattern is repeated together with the hairbrush, to make a focal point for the deep corner design. A smaller rose heads each swag of the border, and finally the rose reappears in the outer corners of the quilt. The concentric circles or

Fig 62

echo quilting in the centre of the roses is repeated between the pierced feathers, giving more definition and emphasis to the enclosed space. Short scrolling lines or curlicues and the fern shapes are all drawn freehand to fill in the remaining spaces.

So here we have a quilt measuring approximately 100×100 inches (250×250 cm), in which only five or six patterns have been used to compose the design. There is good contrast between the straight lines of the background and the flowing curves of the main patterns. There are changes in proportion or scale of the rose and fern patterns, and there is a pleasing overall balance between the main pattern areas and the background.

USING BASIC PRINCIPLES

We see basic design principles – simplicity, balance, contrast, value, repetition – in the quilt on page 88.

The original design was worked out from a rough sketch of overlapping circles. Figs 63a and b on page 89 show two of the centre motifs which developed from the initial idea. These illustrate the almost limitless possibilities waiting to be discovered in one pattern. The corners were adapted from a section of the central design, and the contrast and balance was provided with crosshatching of differing proportion or scale. The scrolling infills of the main pattern were drawn freehand directly onto the quilt top, completing a successful controlled arrangement of one simple idea. A comparison of the first quick sketch and the finished quilt in the photograph gives an impressive indication of the gap between them.

From this quilt we can see that it is possible to construct a good medallion design using only one shape or idea in varying proportions. Experiment with the simple leaf

Many patterns were considered in the planning of this boldly coloured wholecloth quilt (left) designed and made by Jane Arthur

Fig 63a

Fig 63b

shape found so often in the Welsh tradition. Figs 6
c, d, e and f show a medallion-style development o
shape which may spark off some ideas of your ow

You might think the strippy style of design, where
patterns are linear and unbroken, is easier and l
problematic. There are no corners to resolve, no gra
pling with the finer points of mathematics encountered i
the medallion style. Good strippy designs are, however,
deceptively simple. The sheer simplicity of a strippy quilt
requires that the patterns should balance and contrast
well. Traditionally, strippy quilts had five, seven or nine

Fig 64a

Fig 64b   *Fig 64c*

An early 20th-century strippy quilt (right), and a detail (above) showing a rose in a square

joined strips of fabric up to 9 inches (22.9 cm) in width. The patterns were often large in scale and simple in outline, but made interesting secondary patterns.

In the quilt shown here, we can see good contrast and balance between the running feather pattern, the rose in a square and the plait. All three patterns are based on curves of varying scale, from the shallow curves of the plait to the tighter curves of the feather edge. Contrast comes from the square surrounding the rose, and from the background quilting. Notice the thoughtfulness of this background quilting – two differing sets of lines have been alternated to excellent effect.

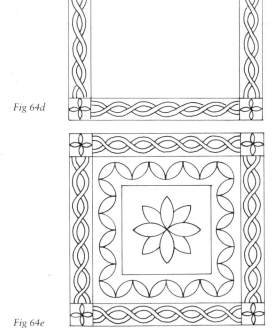

Fig 64d

Fig 64e   *Fig 64f*

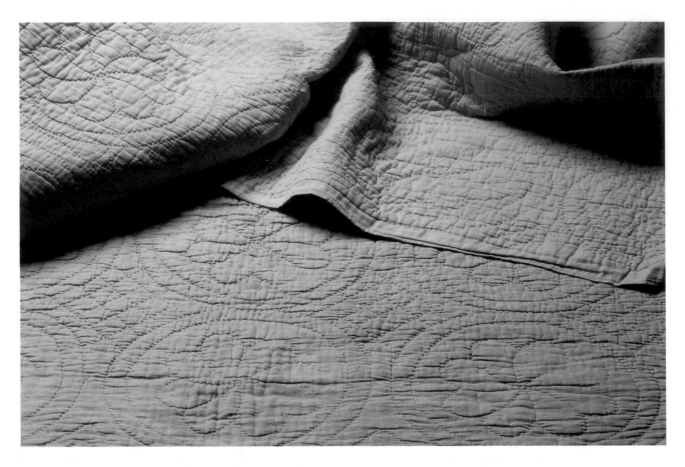

An 'everyday' quilt with an all-over quilting pattern showing a double ring around a rose

By using the leaf shape again, a basic strippy quilt plan can be built up. Fig 65 may start you thinking about possible combinations and arrangements.

While it is possible for a quilt to have an allover design, there are very few examples for us to study. The much-used quilt shown here has only one pattern repeated in an allover style. While this quilt adheres to the design principles of simplicity and repetition, the absence of contrast results in a lacklustre appearance. Allover quilting patterns were frequently used for patchwork and appliqué quilts and can also be seen in many contemporary quilts. In both instances allover pattern gives texture without intrusion.

Fig 65

ASYMMETRICAL DESIGNS

In an asymmetrical design, there should not be too much visual weight in any one area. Balance is the key to success.

Some excellent pioneering work in this style has increased our awareness of its possibilities, and many Japanese quilters show a natural affinity for balanced asymmetry in their work. Try using the now-familiar leaf shape to give you a feel for this style of design. If this style appeals to you, books on Far Eastern decorative art will furnish you with more ideas than you can handle!

In the quilt shown opposite a pattern normally found filling in background space has pride of place. Simple lines make the shapes formed by the overlapping circles into stylised leaves. Balance and contrast are provided by a

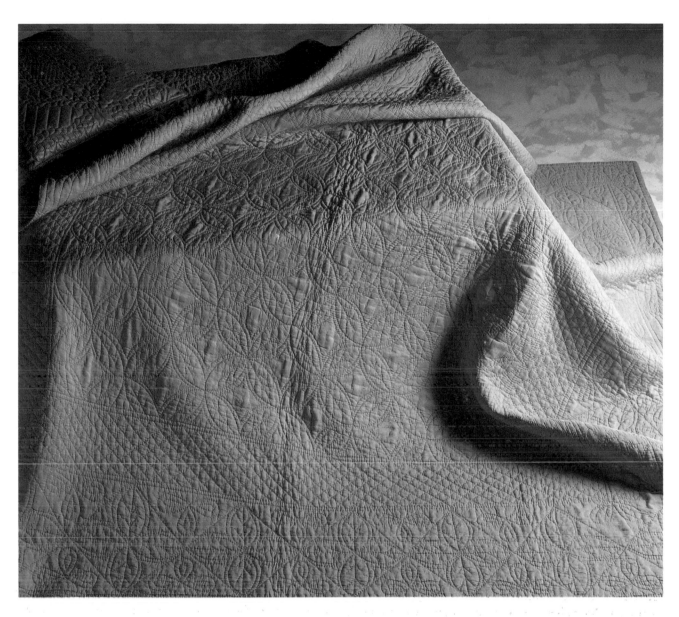

Gold shantung quilt with a simple design

border of crosshatching separated from the central area by a double line of quilting. The next border contrasts well, but is still based on the centre pattern – four of the leaf shapes have become a single unit neatly enclosed in a square (Fig 66a). Both the centre (Fig 66b) and one border (Fig 66c) share the same pattern (with a little variation) and the delicate outer border with its small swags and fans makes a lovely final contrast (Fig 66d).

Fig 66a

Fig 66b

Fig 66c

Fig 66d

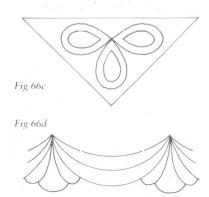

The overall spareness of this quilt inspired one student to make a quilt using only one motif. The burning question was which motif to use. None of the traditional patterns seemed quite right, but after much agonised and laboured drawing, inspiration finally came: a trefoil shape (Fig 67) roughed out on a scrap of paper developed into the rich but simple design shown in the photograph here.

The trefoil shape was used large-scale to make four square units for the centre, a separating border of close crosshatching balanced and contrasted with the larger curves, and the trefoil, much reduced, was then repeated in the outer border. The basic motif would, with a little background quilting, make a handsome cushion design.

The principles of simplicity, balance, contrast, value and repetition provide useful guidelines when you plan your own designs and help develop your quilting 'eye' as you look at the wealth of quilting patterns that exist.

Cream-coloured quilt designed and made by Margaret Salt, who found inspiration using a single trefoil shape in differing proportions

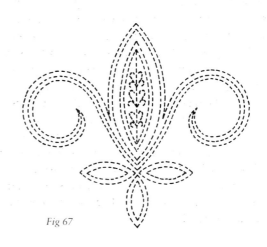

Fig 67

Chapter Seven

FEATHERS AND CABLES

FEATHERED PATTERNS

*W*hen and where did feathered quilting patterns originate? It is possible that these patterns with their perennial appeal were adapted from woodcarving patterns; many of the feather quilting patterns handed down in America and England show a remarkable similarity to carved decoration. Whatever their beginnings, feather patterns have been, and still are, much favoured for quilts. The exuberant beauty of large feathered shapes on early colonial wholecloth quilts contrasts with the refined and elegant feathered wreaths and swags which often accompanied elaborate appliqué patterns on later quilts. Feathers of all sizes and descriptions are found in abundance in the tradition of the North East of England, ranging from the overblown fancifulness of George Gardiner's patterns (Fig 68) to the more tightly controlled feathered twist (Fig 77, page 98).

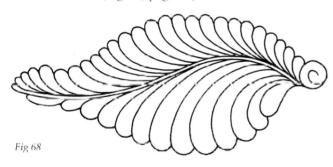

Fig 68

Scrolling feather borders are featured on many Amish quilts, where they show to excellent advantage within the stark framework of sombre colours and strong geometric lines. The Princess Feather, a popular appliqué pattern in the 1840s, probably encouraged even wider use of feather quilting patterns. The frequent use of feather patterns on masterpiece quilts led to a deep-rooted quilting myth. Feathers, it is said, are only for the experienced quilter and are appallingly complicated to stitch. Nothing could be further from the truth, and drawing feathers to suit your own requirements is much easier than you think.

All feathers are essentially one line which is the centre or spine, and either one or two outer parallel lines which are scalloped, with the scallops connected to the central line with short curving lines. Once you look at feather patterns in this way, the whole drafting process is much easier to understand.

DRAFTING FEATHER PATTERNS

Begin by tracing feather patterns such as the one in Fig 95a on page 105 to help you to get a feel for the curves which make up the feather loops. First trace the spine, then work along the loops on each side. Don't rush; try to draw each loop in a single smooth movement without lifting the pencil from the paper. Start each loop either from the spine or the outer edge as you prefer – one direction may feel more natural than the other. Make as many tracings as you like – soon you will be drawing loops with ease. Build on this skill by drawing feathers at every opportunity.

One of the simplest ways to draw feathers is to make a notched tear-drop shape template (Fig 69a). If you study

Fig 69a

feather patterns, you will see that each of the feather's loops resembles a tear drop and by repeatedly laying the template down along a central spine and drawing around it, a feathered line can be built up (Fig 69b).

Fig 69b

This method can be slow but will give you confidence if you belong to the 'can't draw' school of thought. For the daring and courageous, here's a more individual way of making feather patterns. Use a flexicurve (available from art shops and most general stationers) to draw the spine of the feather, or draw it freehand. Draw dotted lines on either side of the spine. Now draw the outer curves of the feather loops using a small circular object such as a coin as a guide (Fig 70).

Fig 70

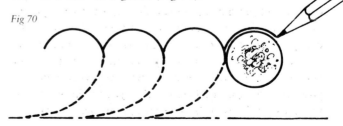

Don't be too concerned about precision and accuracy – the lines can be amended and tidied up afterwards.

It doesn't matter if the curves are not all the same size or distance from the spine. Irregular feather loops are often more lively and appealing than perfectly regular ones. Complete the loops freehand, working either from the spine outwards or from the curves inwards to meet the spine. Experiment with making some of the loops smaller and thinner than others. If the connecting lines are too short, the feather will look squat rather than elegant and flowing (Fig 71).

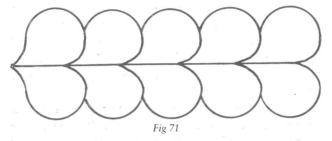

Fig 71

Once you relax and let your eye guide your hand, you will be surprised how easy and adaptable this method can be. Use a soft-lead pencil (2B) and keep the pencil point on the paper as much as possible – your lines will be more confident and flowing as a result. Individual and customised feathers drawn to fit particular spaces are now within your grasp. With a little practice you will be able to draw feathers without the help of the 'tools', or by drawing around your thumb (Fig 72).

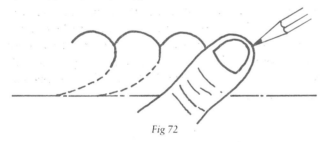

Fig 72

Be prepared to smooth out and amend some of the lines afterwards, remembering that it is acceptable to have feathers with non-identical loops . . . the type of feather and its construction is your choice. Practise the methods outlined above and enjoy making your own patterns. Try drawing feathers with loops which travel from right to left as well as left to right, or those with separate or singular loops (Fig 73).

If you have any stencils for feathers in your pattern collection, try adapting them. Commercial stencils are

Fig 73

often made up of identical, very formal feather loops – make the design a little more individual by drawing the spine and outer curves from the stencil and then filling in the connecting lines freehand.

FEATHER WREATHS

Formal feather wreaths are more exacting to draft, but not difficult. Think of the wreath as three concentric circles: the middle circle is the spine and both inner and outer circles are each subdivided into scallops. Obviously, there will have to be more scallops around the outer circle because of the greater circumference. All scallops join up to the spine with a repeated arc or curved line.

You can draft feather wreaths of any size without compasses and protractor by folding paper. To begin, you need lightweight paper such as greaseproof or typing paper. Draw around a plate or other circular object which is approximately the required size. Fold the paper into quarters, then eighths and possibly sixteenths as shown in Figs 74a and b.

Cut one symmetrical curve across the wide end of the folded wedge and a second curve across the narrow end. Make a small straight cut on both sides of the wedge approximately halfway between the two curved edges as shown in Fig 74c.

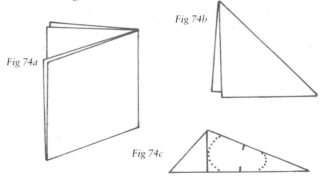

Fig 74a   *Fig 74b*

Fig 74c

Unfold the paper carefully to reveal an outline feather wreath complete with guide marks for the spine. Connect the scalloped edges to the spine freehand, remembering to keep all these lines moving in the same direction around the wreath (Fig 74d).

Fig 74d

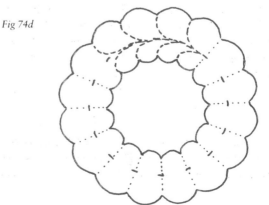

A second geometry-free way of drafting a feathered wreath also involves drawing a circle on lightweight paper. Cut out the circle, fold carefully into quarters, and then unfold. Mark and cut out a narrow strip of thin card (cereal packet is fine) which is the radius of the circle.

With the card strip in position on the circle as shown in Fig 75, mark the edge of the strip to indicate the spine and the inside of the wreath. Now move the marked strip around the circle carefully; keep it steady in the centre and mark pencil guide lines on the paper as you go. You should finish with a paper circle showing dotted lines for the spine and inner edge. Draw scallops and curved lines to connect the line of the spine. Again, keep the loops moving in the same direction around the circle.

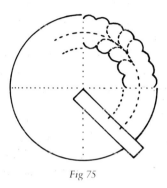

Fig 75

Feathers can be one or two-sided. Try offsetting the connecting lines so that they do not meet at the spine as they do in Fig 71. This will make the feather look more fluid and appealing. Also, take care not to reverse the direction of the joining lines in an 'S' shape, as in Fig 76;

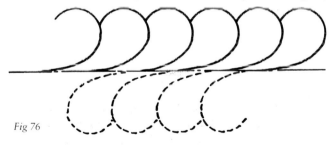

Fig 76

think of an irregular curved 'm' shape instead. It may be easier to work the feathering in the same direction as the original spine was drawn: if you drew the line from left to right, then begin connecting up the feathers at the left. If you plan to have tapering feathers, try beginning feathering where the loops will be smallest and work back along the line.

RUNNING FEATHER

Continuous feather borders are most satisfying to draft. Measure two pieces of shelf-lining or similar paper to the length and width of the quilt. Use a flexicurve to draw the

repeating curve, or fold the paper in half, then quarters and possibly eighths and then draw the curve for the spine freehand onto the folded paper. The feather can then be filled in using one of the methods already described.

Once you have drawn your first feather pattern, take a few moments to experiment with the mirror technique outlined in Chapter Eight. You may discover additional feather patterns which harmonise and combine with the one you have just drafted. See if you can develop a corner unit, a small motif and perhaps the beginnings of a medallion pattern.

Running or continuous feathers can flow in one direction around the border, or they can be reversed at each corner and at the midpoint of the sides. Additional motifs can enhance or disguise joins. If you prefer to reverse the motifs, you need to draw only one complete quarter on your Master Sheet.

To make templates of a feather pattern, punch holes at intervals along the spine as guide marks for transferring the pattern onto fabric. Of course, a hole punched in all of your quilting templates means they can be kept together on a keyring or hook to avoid losing them.

CORNERS

Turning a running feather pattern around corners can be easily achieved with the use of a mirror placed at 45° to the pattern. This will help you to visualise the final effect and make any alterations that may be necessary to the pattern curves. Remember that the mirror reverses the pattern it reflects, so the feathers appear to flow away from the corner. You can use the reflection just to see how the curves turn the corner, or to plan the pattern with some accuracy. (See Chapter Eight for a full discussion of using mirrors.)

REVERSING

If you decide to reverse the direction of a feather pattern at, say, the corners and perhaps also the midpoint of each side, you might consider using an additional motif to make these points a feature – hearts blend well, although there are many other possibilities. When you have worked out where and how the pattern can be reversed, you are still free to adapt the original pattern by omitting or altering some of the lines close to the reversing point, instead of having some unsightly overcrowded lines.

FEATHER TWIST

This combination of feather and cable produces an immensely appealing pattern which always appears satisfyingly complex!

The basis of the pattern is a cable template of appropriate size – see page 100 for drafting cables. Beginning with this template, lightly mark in the 'eye' of the cable. Fill in one side of the cable with evenly spaced lines, then 'feather' the second side by working from a central line (Fig 77).

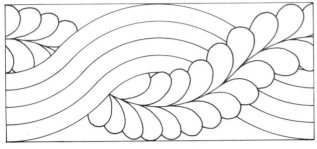

Fig 77

Be careful to maintain the 'under-and-over' weaving of the pattern lines and take care when turning corners. Both feather and lines should turn or be accounted for, but partial or incomplete loops are allowed. Again, it is possible to use a motif at any point where the pattern will be reversed, such as corners and midpoints.

FEATHERED HEARTS AND OTHER SHAPES

Draw half the heart on folded tracing paper. Feather this line and then trace through onto the second fold of paper. Hearts and other shapes can be subtly defined by the use of a double line for the spine.

For symmetrical shapes, try drawing one half of the shape on tracing paper, then flip it over (Fig 78a).

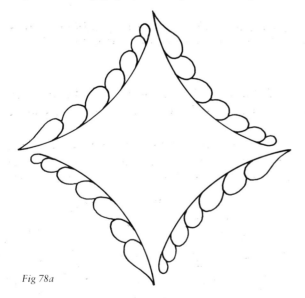

Fig 78a

If you prefer, draw the full shape and take the feathering around it in one direction only (Figs 78b). This works best for an asymmetrical shape (Fig 78c).

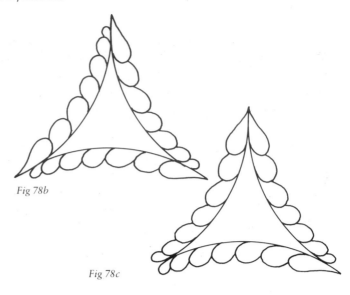

Fig 78b

Fig 78c

Feather patterns offer much scope for combining the trapunto and cording techniques discussed in Chapter Five. The central spine can be doubled to make a channel for cording, and individual feather loops can be further enhanced by additional stuffing.

Spaces enclosed by feathered lines can be filled with close quilting such as small-scale crosshatching (Fig 79). The photograph shows the rich texture and good contrast that emphasise the curves of the feathers.

Fig 79

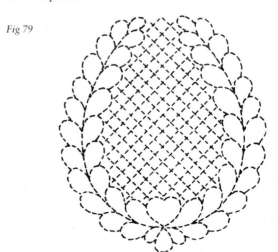

QUILTING FEATHERS

Feather patterns are among the most enjoyable of all to quilt. They are, however, slower than straight line patterns because of the need to change direction frequently. There is no single correct quilting sequence for feathers, but the suggestions below may be helpful when you begin. Quilt along the spine first and then stitch the loops as indicated by the arrows, 'floating' from one to the other as necessary (see page 33). Keep moving in one direction consistent with the direction of the feathered line (Fig 80).

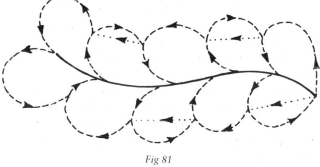

Fig 80

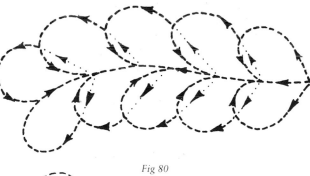

Close quilting such as the crosshatching (grid) filling the space between the two feathers on this pink quilt provides rich texture

Instead of working first one side and then the other, you could try stitching one loop and then its opposite as in Fig 81.

Large-scale feathers can have the spine worked first, followed by the outer scalloped lines. The loops can then be completed with curved 'm' lines as shown in Fig 82.

Fig 81

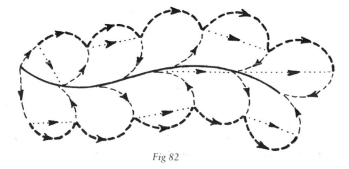

Fig 82

to develop hammocks and swags by working with only one side of a basic template and offsetting the curved lines.

QUILTING SEQUENCE FOR CABLES

Like feathers, there is no single correct sequence to follow when quilting cables. However, it is advisable to approach the quilting methodically. For a simple cable you could stitch in either of the ways shown in Figs 92a and b.

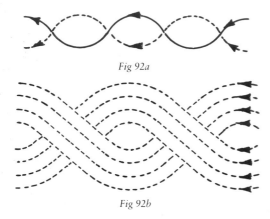

Fig 92a

Fig 92b

Lined twist cables can be quilted one line at a time with a single needle or you could work with one needle for each line of pattern, taking a few stitches along each line so that the whole pattern is completed before moving on. The one line at a time approach may prove less disruptive to the quilting rhythm, but the multi-needle method allows the whole pattern to be worked progressively, which can seem quicker.

PROJECT: FIRST FEATHER CUSHION

Finished cushion 15 inches (37.5 cm) square

TECHNIQUES

Master Sheet
Tacking
Marking quilt pattern
Quilting

YOU WILL NEED

18 in. (45 cm) square of top fabric
20 in. (50 cm) square of 2 oz. wadding
   (batting)
20 in. (50 cm) square of backing fabric
18 in. (45 cm) square of fabric
   for cushion back
Tracing or shelf paper

Fig 93

Ruler, pencil, black felt-tip pen, eraser
Fabric marker (test for removal)
Tacking (basting) thread
Thread to match top fabric
Betweens needles of your choice
Hoop, tubular frame or small traditional frame

1 Trace the pattern given in Fig 93 on page 102 and make a Master Sheet, indicating centre lines and corners with a heavily dashed line.

2 Press top and backing fabrics, then measure and lightly mark the central horizontal, vertical and diagonal lines and the outer edges of the design area onto the top fabric.

3 Tape the Master Sheet on a smooth surface and position the top fabric over it with tape, matching up the guide marks.

4 Trace the design on the top fabric using your chosen marker. Check that you have traced all the lines before removing the tape from fabric and Master Sheet.

5 Centre the top fabric over the backing and wadding (batting) and tack (baste) all three layers together following the usual sequence (see pages 28 and 29).

6 Quilt using matching thread and working in a systematic sequence.

7 Measure and trim the quilted square and make up into a cushion cover using your preferred method.

PROJECT: CABLE AND RUNNING FEATHER STRIPPY QUILT

This large-scale project includes both feathers and cables. The quilt will measure approximately 74×87 inches (185×217.5 cm) when finished.

TECHNIQUES

Making cable templates
Measuring and balancing repeats for feather
Tracing patterns
Direct marking with template
Tacking
Quilting
Binding or front to back finished edges

YOU WILL NEED

2½ yds. (2.25 m) each of two contrasting plain (solid) fabrics 45 in. (112.5 cm) wide – dressweight 100% cotton is ideal

77×90 in. (192.5×225 cm) (minimum) 2 oz. wadding (batting)
4½ yds. (4 m) backing fabric
Ruler, pencil, black felt-tip marker, eraser
Plastic or card for making template
Tracing paper
Fabric marker(s) (test for removal)
Tacking (basting) thread
Threads to match each top fabric
Betweens needles of your choice
Hoop, tubular frame or
    traditional quilting frame

1 Cut the two top fabrics into strips as follows: 4 strips of one fabric measuring 11×88 inches (27.5×220 cm), 2 strips of contrasting fabric to the same measurement and 1 strip contrasting fabric 15×88 inches (37.5×220 cm). Seam strips together with the widest strip in the centre. Press seams open; then press the whole top. Set aside.

2 If necessary, seam backing fabric together to measure a minimum 77×90 inches (192.5×225 cm) – larger would be better. Make sure that none of the seam lines coincide

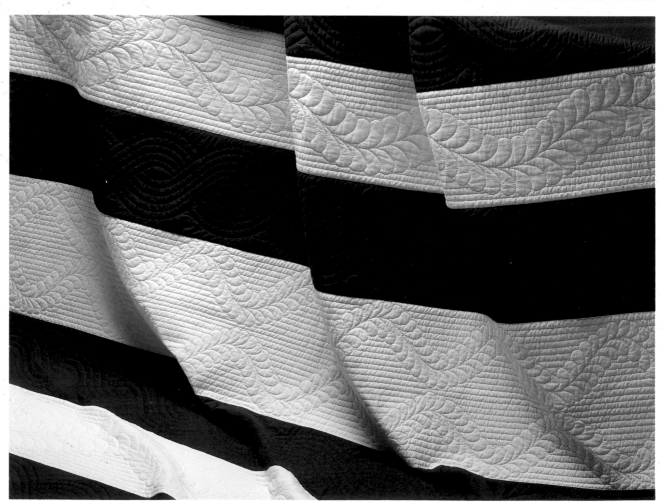

Fig 95a

with the seam lines on the quilt top. Press seams open, then press the backing and set aside.

3 Make any necessary joins in the wadding (batting) and spread it out flat to eliminate creases.

4 Trace the cable pattern (Fig 94) on pages 106 and 107 and make a template. You may find it helpful to make slits or holes at intervals along the inner lines to guide you when completing the pattern.

5 Trace the two feather patterns (Figs 95a and b) on this page and pages 108 and 109 and make templates if you wish. Alternatively use the pattern sections given to build up two Master Sheet strips of 10×87 inches (25×217.5 cm) for the side strips and 14×87 inches (35×217.5 cm) for the centre panel.
Note: These instructions assume placement of the feather patterns on the paler of the two contrasting fabrics. If you wish to reverse the pattern placement, you need to make a template for the feather patterns. Better still, draft your own feathers using one of the methods outlined in this chapter.

6 Using the template and the two Master Sheet strips, mark the cable and feather patterns on the quilt top. You may need a different-coloured marker for each fabric.

7 Centre all three layers carefully and tack (baste) together in the usual sequence.

8 Begin quilting either from the centre of the quilt or from one corner and along one edge (see page 35).

9 When the quilting is complete, remove all tacking (basting) and markings and either bind the edges or bring the backing over to the front as described in Chapter Three.

10 Label and photograph the quilt before use!

the bed where it will be lost to view. The central design should fit comfortably into, say, a 48-inch (120-cm) square, with background and borders filling the remaining space. Borders for double quilts probably need to be a minimum of 6 inches (15 cm) in depth. Anything less makes the border look like a hasty afterthought, out of balance with the main design. Borders of 10 to 12 inches (25 to 30 cm) are most effective on a project of this size. There are no firm rules about scale. You may find it easier to begin with an understanding of what is too small and work from there. It can be quite a shock to be confronted with the size of patterns for full-size quilts if you have only looked at designs for cushions and crib quilts.

ENLARGING AND REDUCING

Photocopiers that enlarge and reduce have removed some of the agony of drawing patterns to different scales. However you should check the final results for accuracy; distortion occurs with both processes. It is useful to understand how to scale patterns up and down using the grid system (see Fig 60, page 84). You may feel you can do better without the grid – you're probably right. Experiment with a pantograph, Fig 97, available from art and office suppliers. Once you have the confidence to work entirely freehand, your results will have more personality than an accurately copied and scaled pattern.

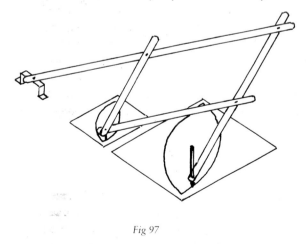

Fig 97

PAPER CUTOUTS

Traditional quilters made and adapted patterns as a matter of course. The well-known quotation of 'worrying with scissors and brown paper' describes an easy and commendable approach to resolving various problems of scale. Many quilters trying to decide how large or small quilting patterns should be feel more comfortable looking at paper cutouts laid out on a bed or flat surface. Cut out a variety and quantity of pattern shapes and move them around to help you visualise a total design.

Not every design decision needs to be taken before you begin to quilt. Many quilts dictate their own terms, so be prepared to adapt and revise as you go along. This flexible approach was used particularly by Welsh quilters, many of whom set up a frame and began to quilt with no precise idea of which patterns they would use.

Plan-as-you-quilt is probably easier if you are working on a large traditional frame and have enough confidence to take risks. Start by placing a motif, singly or combined, in one corner; then match up the other corner. Add filler and borders. Decide on a centrepiece; then repeat everything for the other half. Sounds easy doesn't it?

QUILTED VS. UNQUILTED SPACE

While you are gaining confidence in drawing patterns and lines, remember that ultimately it is the spaces between the lines of stitching that give a design much of its impact. As you work through the decisions that help design a quilt, stop from time to time and look at the spaces being created between the drafted lines. Do they all appear to be the same? If so, consider varying the scale and proportion. Are the spaces between the main pattern the same as those between the lines of background? The background may be more effective with more closely spaced lines to contrast with the unquilted spaces of the main pattern.

DESIGN EXERCISE

Pick up a leaf with an interesting shape and trace around it. Cut out as many paper shapes as you can bear to, varying the size and scale, and try arranging them in a border design or a centre medallion.

If you used oak leaves, you could perhaps include some acorns in your drawings. The background quilting could be crosshatched, or you could imitate woodgrain or tree rings. Try arranging the same paper cutouts asymmetrically. Can you make a linear pattern from the same shapes which would be suitable for a strippy quilt? Try and see. You do not need to work on a grand scale – a 12 to 16-inch (30 to 40-cm) square will be sufficient.

Fig 98 shows some of the steps involved in developing a single feathered line into a complete quilt design. The feather drawn in full on page 113 is represented in Fig 99 by a stylised 'm' symbol. Dotted lines indicate further possibilities from the same feather. Look at this illustration in conjunction with Fig 99; you can see the simple logical steps in the process of building up a complete design from just one motif.

If the scale of the feather were to be varied, perhaps by enlarging it in the centre to two or three times its original size, the final design would be more interesting.

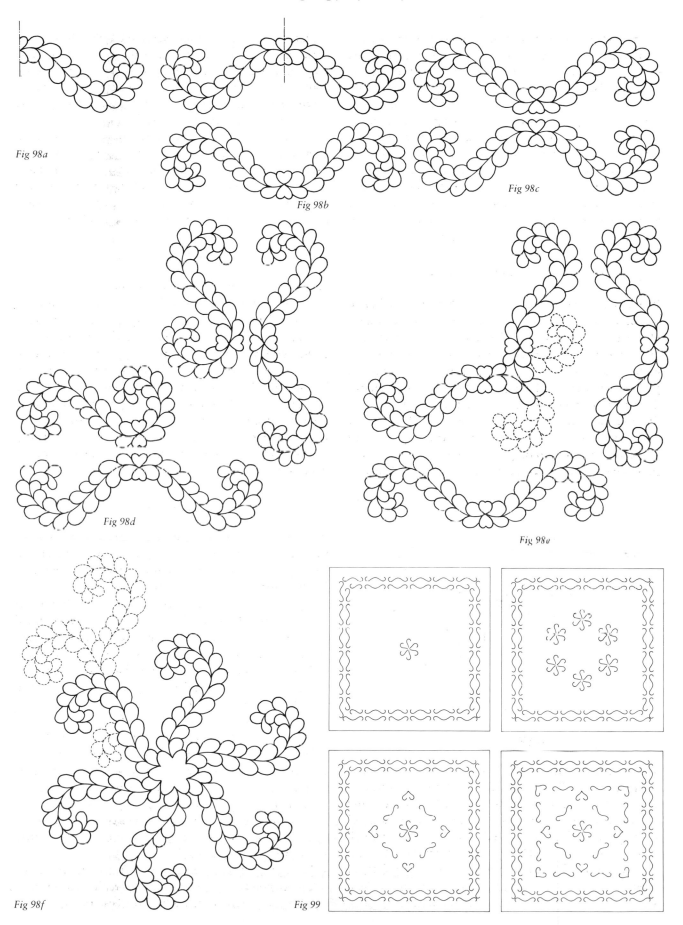

Fig 98a

Fig 98b

Fig 98c

Fig 98d

Fig 98e

Fig 98f

Fig 99

STRIPPY QUILT DESIGNS

The traditional use of strips of fabric for a quilt top gives a very rigid, spare and deceptively simple framework within which to place the design. Simple, even bold, pattern lines often work best.

The strippy quilt on page 114 has a high contrast between the glazed cotton strips; the quilting patterns have a similar boldness of scale. A single plait has been doubled to fill the width of one strip and the sweep of the feathers contrasts well with both the plait and the rose in a square pattern on the outer strips. A very basic strippy quilt can be seen on page 104. The contrast between navy and white seemed to call for equal simplicity of pattern. The centre strip of two running feathers is the only

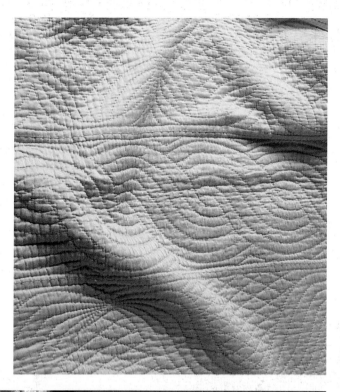

All the quilts shown on these two pages are examples of strippy quilts. The traditional blue and yellow one (left) was made by Gladys Pate. The design on the red and white (below) has been worked with coarse cream thread and large uneven stitches; despite these supposed faults, it is a pleasing quilt. The well-worn 1930s strippy on the right has simple patterns and background quilting – nothing complicated, just lots of appealing texture

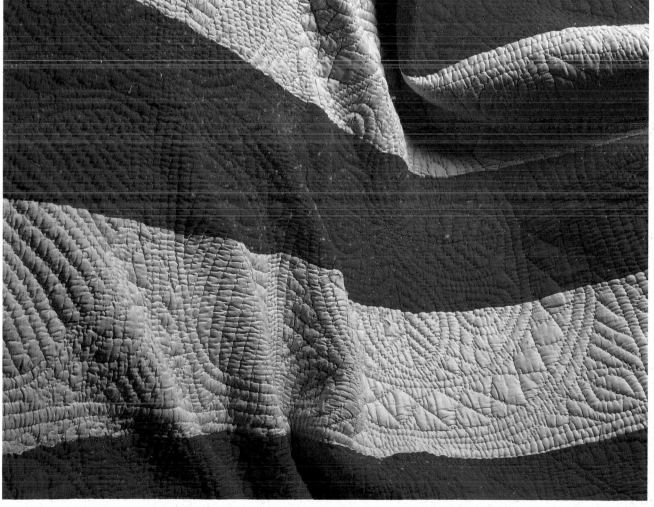

embellishment to the larger-scale running feather and the bold twist of the cable.

There are no rules which say that all strips must be of the same width, although this arrangement is commonly found on old quilts. The pink strippy uses traditional patterns with an arrangement of strips one degree away from the traditional. There is limited colour contrast between the fabrics so the width of the strips has been varied. Although it hardly re-invents the wheel, this may

The width of the strips varies in this contemporary pastel strippy quilt. The wide strips have been quilted with simple patterns, the narrower ones are plain

present other possibilities for arranging strips and patterns. And there is no reason why the design should be confined within the linear structure of a strippy quilt. The red and white quilt on page 115 has a bold medallion design which completely disregards the pieced strips.

A quilt in progress, designed by Janet Heaney using mirrors on a curled feather pattern

THE MAGIC OF MIRRORS

The use of mirrors for predicting pattern repeats for patchwork is well established. It is much quicker and easier to sew or draw one block and view it in two mirrors to gain some idea of how several will look when repeated. For any symmetrical design only one quarter or one half need be drawn out and then checked with a mirror.

This simple design device using mirrors or mirror tiles is fascinating to try on quilting patterns both traditional and modern, and more thought-provoking than a kaleidoscope. It will also give you more hours of fun and inspiration than you would have dreamed possible. In Fig 100 on pages 118 and 119, you can see what happens when a simple feathered line is reflected.

Fig 100 shows how mirrors predict new pattern arrangements. Try this for yourself by tracing a favourite motif and sliding a sheet of white paper under the tracing to enhance the contrast of the lines. Now hold the mirrors in place anywhere on the motif. Alter the angle by opening and closing the mirrors; slide them backwards and forwards over the whole motif and see what happens.

The mirror technique was advocated as long ago as

Two mirrors and a simple feather design can produce a number of variations

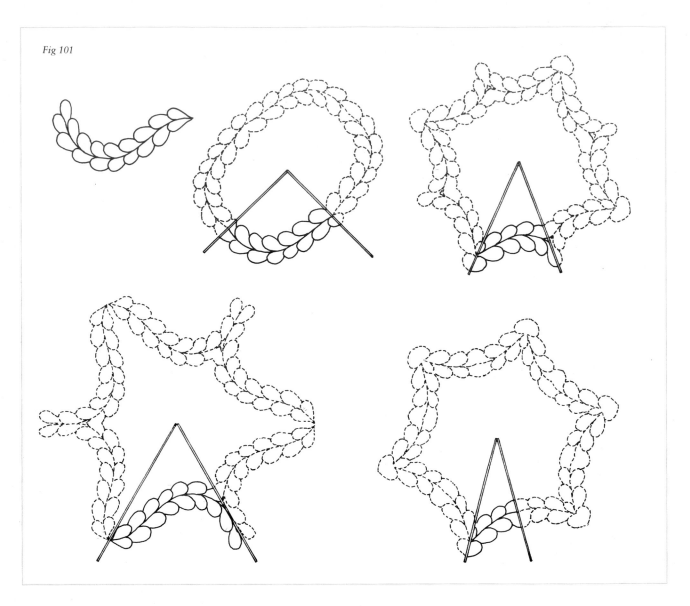

Fig 101

led lines as you discover more and more pleasing reflections. One sure way of capturing them all is to stop and trace each segment, together with its boundary lines, as it appears. Do not trust to memory, but trace it there and then!

MIRRORED CORNERS

The very least that this technique can offer is help in planning graceful corners. Hold one mirror at a 45° angle to a tracing of your border design and slide it along to find the best way to turn the design at the corner. Lightly mark this with pencil along the bottom edge of the mirror, pick up the tracing and fold carefully along this marked line. Now retrace the design and unfold; your design is ready.

When you are working with cutout paper shapes, mirrors can help to predict pattern repeats and to develop other shapes and combinations.

Don't be afraid to use your mirrors on 'odd' segments

of any pattern (Fig 101). Some of the best results come in this way. Keep moving the mirrors along random sections of your pattern at any angle. It doesn't matter if the angle of the mirrors is not a perfect 90°, 45°, 30°. You probably won't want to use every single line in the reflection, sometimes an overall shape is pleasing, but some of the lines need erasing or amending.

The more you play with this method of adapting and predicting patterns, the easier it becomes to see possibilities. You will soon be manipulating and combining patterns with skill and confidence. When you arrive at a new pattern unit, don't just record it and file it away – use the mirrors on this new unit, both as a whole and on random segments. You may find even more pattern gems just waiting to be discovered!

A yellow quilt in progress and a choice of designs worked out by its maker, Margaret Philbin

PROJECT: LARGE WHOLECLOTH QUILT

Here's a chance to test your skills in marking and quilting on a grand scale by re-creating the quilt shown.
Finished quilt measures approx. 82×95 inches (205×237.5 cm)

TECHNIQUES

Preparing fabrics and wadding
Tacking
Use of Master Sheet and/or templates
Background quilting
Freehand marking
Sides-to-middle finish of edges

YOU WILL NEED

Top: 5½ yds. (5 m) 45 in. (112.5 cm) wide fabric – polished cotton would look good
2 oz. wadding (batting) – either prepared king-size or widths of 2 oz. wadding (batting) joined to a minimum of 84×97 in. (210×242.5 cm)
Backing: 5½ yds. (5 m) of 45 in. (112.5 cm) wide fabric – plain (solid), not print
Long ruler/yardstick
Masking tape
Fabric marker (remember to test first)
Plastic or card to make templates
Tracing paper
Black felt-tipped marker, pencil, eraser
Thread to match top fabric
Betweens needles of your choice
Hoop, tubular frame or traditional frame

METHOD

1 Seam together the top fabric to measure 84×97 in. (210×242.5 cm)
Use one full width for the centre panel with half or full widths on each side.
Remember that the top should be larger than the complete design area of the quilt to allow for finishing edges, etc. Press seams open, then press the complete top and set aside.

2 Seam together the backing fabric to measure a minimum 84×97 in. (210×242.5 cm) using two full widths of fabric if possible. This avoids having seams too close to each other which can make quilting difficult.
Press these seams open, then press the complete backing and set aside.

3 If you are not using prepared wadding (batting), butt and join together wadding to the required size.
Note: It is important that all three layers of the quilt should be larger than the measurements of the completed quilt. In particular, both backing and wadding (batting) should be at least 2 inches (5 cm) larger than the top on all four sides.

4 Mark centre lines on the top fabric, then measure and lightly mark the diagonals. Also mark lines for the finished edge of the quilt and a 45° angle at each corner.

5 Trace all the patterns (Figs 102a, b, c, d, e, f, g and h) and make templates from plastic or card.

6 Direct marking method
  a Position and secure one quarter of the top on a clean surface.
  b Using the diagram in Fig 62, page 87, to check placement, position and mark around the templates to outline the main patterns. Fill in the details of the outlined shapes freehand, using only the lightest pressure. Feel free to change or substitute any other patterns at this point if you wish to add your own touch of individuality.
  c On the original quilt the fern shapes and curlicues are drawn freehand – practise drawing both on scraps of paper until you feel ready to draw straight onto the quilt top.
  d The background crosshatching can be added at this stage if you wish – use a long ruler or yardstick. Alternatively, mark just a few lines as a guide for placing masking tape once you have begun to quilt.

7 Tracing method
If the prospect of marking directly onto fabric does not appeal you may prefer to make a Master Sheet and trace the design through if your fabric is suitable.
  a Tape shelf or tracing paper together to measure slightly more than one quarter of the size of the finished quilt.
  b Mark horizontal, vertical and diagonal lines at one corner of the paper with a heavy dotted line. These represent one quarter of the centre lines. Similarly, mark lines to show where the finished edges will be, and measure and mark a 45° angle diagonally opposite the centre lines.
  c Again, using Fig 62, page 87, as a guide, position and draw around the templates in pencil, filling in the details freehand.
  d Once you have drawn all the main patterns to your satisfaction, finalise the lines by going over them with a black felt-tipped marker. Use an eraser afterwards to remove any remaining pencil.
  e If you wish, all the background lines can be ruled

Fig 102c

Fig 102d

126

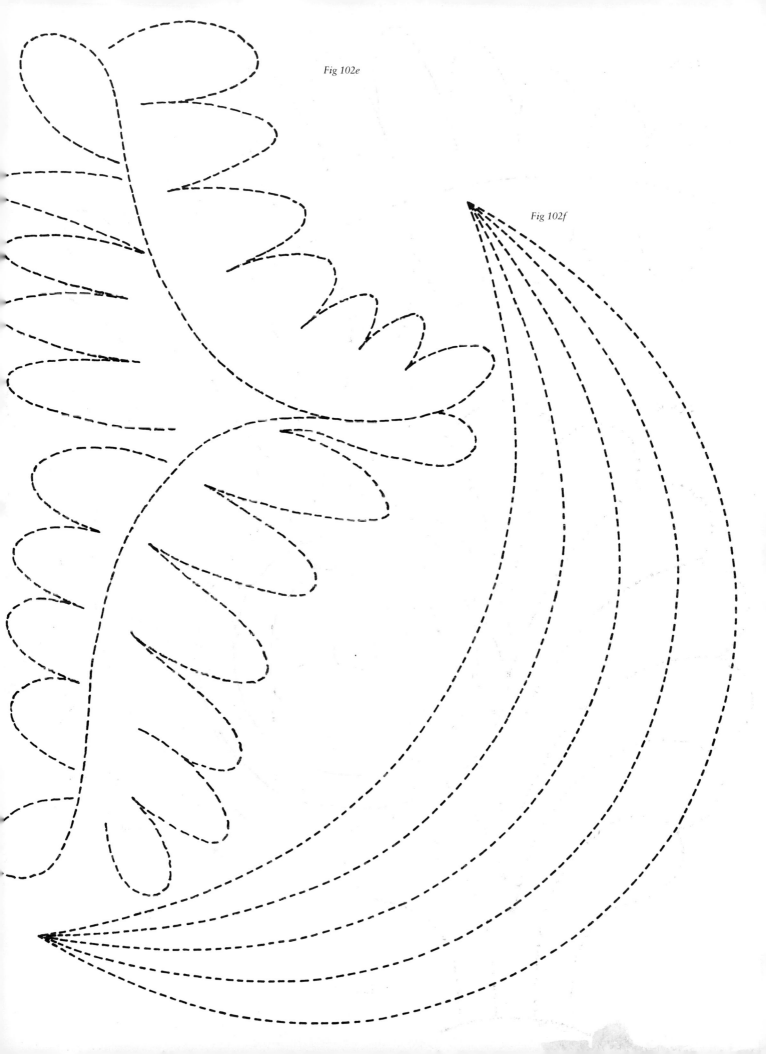

Fig 102e

Fig 102f

Fig 102g

Fig 102h

PROJECT: FEATHER CUSHION

TECHNIQUES

Pattern manipulation
Pattern marking
Quilting

YOU WILL NEED

½ yd. (0.5 m) of 45 in. (112.5 cm) wide fabric
20 in. (50 cm) square of 2 oz. wadding (batting)
20 in. (50 cm) square of backing fabric
Betweens needles of your choice
Thread to match
Beeswax (optional)
Portable quilting frame (optional)

Fabric marker of your choice
Tracing/layout paper and pencil
Black felt-tipped marker

1 Trace the patterns in Figs 103a and b from page 130 onto two separate pieces of tracing paper.

2 Draw a 17-inch (42.5-cm) square on a third sheet of tracing paper – this will be the Master Sheet. Measure and mark the centre, horizontal, vertical and diagonal lines.

3 Slide the patterns into various positions underneath the Master Sheet and use one or two mirrors to help you visualise the effect (see page 117).

4 Even if you decide to follow the pattern arrangement of the cushion illustrated, take a little time to experiment and see what other groupings you can devise for yourself.

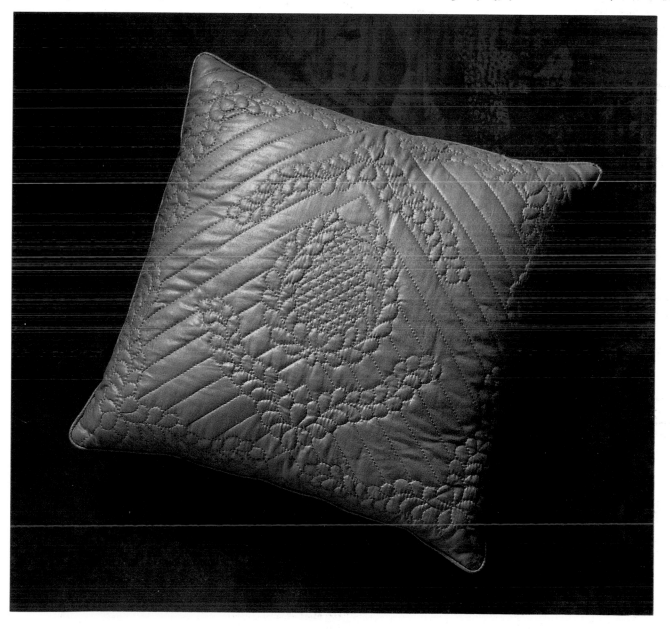

Fig 103a

Fig 103b

5 Once you have made your final choices, fill in the Master Sheet using a black marker.

6 Mark the completed design onto your fabric using whichever method is appropriate (see Chapter Two for full details on marking).

7 With the pattern marked onto the top fabric you are ready to quilt. If you are using a portable hoop or frame, you will need to tack (baste) the layers of top, wadding (batting) and backing together (see pages 28 and 29). If you are working on a small traditional frame, the layers can be set in the frame without further ado.

8 Quilt! Relax and enjoy. (See Chapter Three for how to quilt – relaxation is up to you).

9 Make up into a cushion using your preferred method.

Chapter Nine

QUILT CARE

CLEANING

NEW QUILTS

Your quilt is finished and bound. It may not be visibly dirty, but it is advisable to let it start its working life as clean as possible. A gentle immersion in cool water may be sufficient to loosen and float out any absorbed or hidden dirt. Follow this with a short spin (do **not** wring) and dry flat in indirect heat. If the quilt is very grubby, use a gentle washing agent dissolved in lukewarm water. Again, a short spin and drying away from direct heat are required.

If you have used a blue water-soluble marker, immerse the quilt completely in cold water before proceeding with any other cleaning, or you may find unsightly pale blue blotches re-appearing later. If you spray or sponge, the marks diffuse into the absorbent wadding (batting) and move back to the surface as they dry.

Heat can melt or partially fuse synthetic wadding, so many quilters never iron their work. It is possible to press a quilt lightly, provided that the top and back are cotton fabrics. Set your iron for cotton and steam and VERY lightly glide over the back of the quilt, barely touching the surface. Keep the iron moving. Shake the quilt well and repeat for the other side. Shake the quilt again and leave it to air. Waddings (battings) which are all-cotton, or have a high proportion of cotton, will respond to ironing better than synthetics, but always use the lightest of touches. Heat and steam will not suit silk or wool wadding.

OLD QUILTS

The golden rule when contemplating any action involving an old quilt is – if in doubt, don't. Cleaning causes considerable stress to old quilts, but this needs to be balanced against the long-term damage caused by excessive dirt within the fibres. You should only consider doing the cleaning yourself if you are confident that you are not dealing with a vital piece of quilting heritage. Home cleaning may be appropriate for an all-cotton quilt which shows no signs of undue wear and tear, fraying, broken stitches, etc. Use a gentle, non-biological washing agent in lukewarm water. Only use a washing machine if it is large enough and has a delicates/gentle cycle and a short spin. A quilt is very heavy when wet, and stitches can break despite careful handling.

WASHING A QUILT

If the bath is your only option, run lukewarm water until the bath is no more than a quarter full. Mix in a small amount of washing agent. Spread out an old sheet in the bath to help lift the wet quilt out later. Immerse the quilt without creases or folds. After fifteen minutes, drain the water and remove the quilt by grasping the four corners of the supporting sheet. Put in fresh lukewarm water and replace the sheet and quilt to rinse. You can, with help, wring out some excess water by twisting the ends of the sheet in opposite directions.

Resist the temptation to put the quilt in a tumble dryer on its own – it may emerge shrunken and creased. The best place to dry a quilt is where it will be flat and supported, preferably out of direct sunlight and in a light breeze.

DRY CLEANING

The term dry cleaning is somewhat misleading. It is not dry at all, but involves immersing an article in a vat of chemical. An all-cotton quilt may emerge compressed and stiff. And beware of spot cleaners unless you are absolutely sure of what you are doing.

DYEING AND BLEACHING

Staunch conservationists will be horrified at the thought of bleaching or dyeing an existing quilt. The chemicals involved in dyeing may weaken the fibres and make the quilt more fragile. Bleaching is a less certain process that will also weaken fibres, and residual colour may linger along the lines of quilting. However a successfully dyed quilt will be used and enjoyed rather than stowed away out of sight. Neither measure should be undertaken lightly. Again, you are advised to seek expert advice.

LABELLING QUILTS

One important aspect of caring for quilts, old or new, is labelling and recording information.

The style, technique and content of a label are a matter of personal choice. The vital information which needs to be recorded is:

Title of quilt

Maker of quilt

Date of completion (and beginning, if you can bear to admit how long it took)

Recipient

Place made

An example of label wording for a new quilt might be:

'LILAC FANS'

MADE BY BARBARA CHAINEY

FOR PAT AND MIKE RAW

TO CELEBRATE THEIR 25TH

WEDDING ANNIVERSARY

OCTOBER 1992

STAFFORDSHIRE

MAKING A BASIC LABEL

The quickest and easiest way of making a label is to write the details on a piece of plain fabric using a waterproof pen with a fine point. Or, iron a piece of freezer paper onto the fabric and type on the information using a fabric typewriter ribbon – ideal when you want to include more information on a small label.

FANCY LABELS

An embroidered label is a lovely addition to any quilt. Use one or two strands of embroidery thread to work the lettering and add embellishments, depending on your mood and embroidery skills. Cross stitch can be worked on plain fabric through a piece of waste canvas. Stitch the lettering through the canvas and label fabric and then carefully withdraw the canvas threads one by one. Soak the canvas thoroughly to remove the threads easily.

Print information on the back of a quilt with a custom-made rubber stamp, or buy personalised labels.

Making a miniature block, appliqué pattern or shape used in the quilt top is another attractive way of labelling

Three antique wholecloth quilts in their rightful place

Examples of stitched and written quilt labels

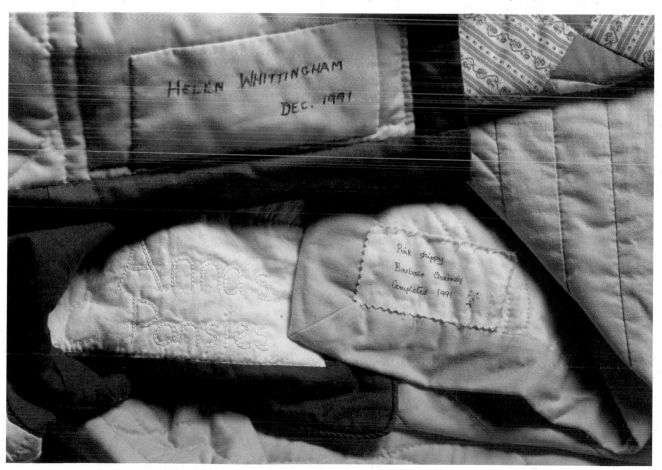

your quilt. For instance, a miniature Ohio Star block could have the necessary information placed in the four corner squares as in Fig 104, while an appliqué pattern could be used in a similar way (Fig 105).

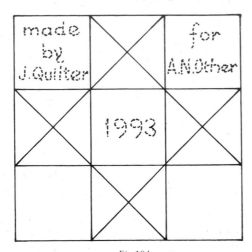

Fig 104

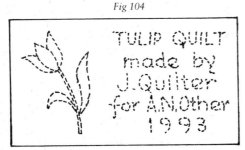

Fig 105

If you are feeling brave, sign your quilt on the front as you would a painting, in either of the lower corners, using a waterproof pen in a contrasting shade, or stitch your name instead. You could even quilt the details somewhere on the quilt itself. However, this is not the most permanent way to identify a quilt. Stitches can break, which will make it difficult to decipher in years to come. So even if you quilt information into your work, it is a good idea to have a label on the back also.

Some quilters keep quilting journals or diaries to help them recall how many hours a quilt took to make and what notable events happened during its progress. Such information will make fascinating reading in years to come and is another commendably Good Habit worth acquiring.

If the quilt is to be given as a gift, a photograph of you with the quilt makes the documentation even more complete. Think how fascinating we find books which show quilts and their makers from years gone by – just try not to imagine how quaint your fashionable clothes or hairstyle will look in years to come! You should photograph all your work for your own memory album anyway, so you can easily have an extra print made to

accompany your quilt.

When you have developed and used patterns from a source other than your own imagination, you should always give credit where it is due. Add to your label information about your starting point.

LABELLING OLD QUILTS

If you have an old quilt bought from a garage sale or handed down through your family, some pertinent facts may remain uncertain. No matter how little information you have, please record what you know on a card and take a photo of the quilt. Keep the card and photograph together in a safe place with other important papers. Ideally, this information should also be attached to the quilt. Labels can be made quickly by writing what you know of the quilt neatly on white or cream fabric with a permanent laundry marker. Don't dismiss the idea of labelling and recording just because the maker and dates are unknown – record how the quilt came to you, your full name, brief address and the date. Try to find out the possible date and name of the pattern as well. Label all *your* work as a matter of course and courtesy to the generations you will not meet.

REPAIRING OLD QUILTS

Badly frayed, ragged and worn quilts are difficult to clean without damaging the fabrics further. In addition, there is the question of how to prevent damage from getting worse. If one area of a quilt has become fragile, one solution is to put a neutral-coloured, closely woven semi-opaque fabric such as net or tulle over the damaged area. Make sure that the net is stitched neatly with matching thread to the stronger fabrics and perhaps baste with tiny stitches through any exposed wadding to the backing.

CRAZY QUILTS

The crazy quilt was found in fashionable households in the late nineteenth century. Thousands must have been made and many excellent examples have survived virtually intact. However, the very nature of a crazy quilt – which included silks, satins, taffeta, linings, velvet, and other fancy scraps – means that some fabrics will have fared better than others. Think carefully before attempting restoration or conservation of this type of quilt. The best advice (you guessed it) is to seek the help of an expert.

The quilting designs on page 137 were taken from this fragment of a badly worn antique strippy quilt and preserved for future use

Where will you find expert advice? Many quilting clubs and guilds operate a heritage and documentation programme and would be delighted to record details of your quilt. They may also be able to offer advice on care, cleaning and conservation. If there is not a group in your area, contact your nearest museum or historical society.

STORAGE

One of the best places for storing quilts is where they belong – on a bed – though this may not be such a good idea if the quilt is old and fragile, or your household includes cats and dogs. Pets seem to have a keen instinct for quilts and many adopt precious specimens as their preferred sleeping quarters. Pets excluded, quilts should ideally be spread out flat and away from direct sunlight. In the absence of space or a pet-proof spare room, quilts can be rolled around a length of dowel or cardboard tube and interlined with acid-free tissue paper. This is ideal for a few quilts, and a high shelf will keep them out of harm's way. Each roll should be covered with a protective cloth casing – washed, unbleached calico (muslin) tied with tapes is best. Never use plastic, which can cause the quilts to sweat and develop mildew and other problems.

If there is no alternative to storing quilts folded on top of each other, take them out frequently to admire and refold. Put acid-free tissue paper between folds if possible. Check for moths occasionally, but **don't** put mothballs between the folds in direct contact with the fabric.

Damaged quilts can be stored where they are visible. Fold over a chair back, blanket chest or the foot of a bed with as much of the damage hidden as possible. This way you can enjoy the quilt without stressing it further, but be careful of direct sunlight, which can fade fabric and make it very fragile.

HANGING QUILTS

Hanging quilts on walls has become increasingly popular. Quilts made specifically as wall decoration should have a fabric sleeve on the back for hanging, but an old quilt will not. Many quilts have been tacked or nailed to walls – with dire results. Tacks, pins and nails should not be used; they can rust and mark the quilt. A large quilt suspended from a line of tacks will develop noticeable holes where the weight of the quilt has pulled against the tacks. A fabric sleeve or loops, which allow a rod or pole to be slipped through, are the best way of supporting the weight of a quilt evenly as it hangs.

Sleeves are simple to make. Cut or join 6 inch (15 cm)-wide lengths of fabric which blend with or match the quilt backing. Fold the strip in half with right sides facing, join the long edges to make a tube (Fig 106a) and turn right side out.

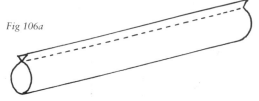

Fig 106a

Hem the raw edges at both ends. Then pin and stitch the sleeve in place on the back of the quilt, making sure your stitches do not go through to the front (Fig 106b).

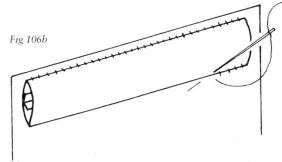

Fig 106b

A temporary sleeve can be made using loops of straight-grain tape held in place with safety pins or small neat stitches. However, this method is not suitable if you want to hang the quilt for a long period, since there is considerable stress where the loops are attached and the pins could mark the fabric.

Be cautious about hanging any quilt, even with a sleeve. Sunlight can fade and weaken fabric, and household dust is bound to settle in the fibres. Dust can be partially removed by vacuuming with the nozzle covered with a fine mesh screen such as muslin (cheesecloth) or old stockings. Steam cleaning units may be too drastic to use on old quilts, as their hot steam can be damaging.

RECORDING PATTERNS

Recording patterns from old quilts which are past their best can be rewarding and is simple to do. The photograph on page 135 shows a very tattered fragment of a strippy quilt; the patterns in Fig 107 opposite and 108 on page 138 were taken from it.

Place tracing paper over the top of the quilt and trace the lines of quilting with a soft pencil. This will give wobbly lines which will need tidying up and redrawing.

If you want to tackle the recording process more professionally, try the piercing method. Take a long fine pin or needle and sink the head firmly into a cork to make it easier to handle. On a smooth, clean surface spread out

Fig 107

Fig 108

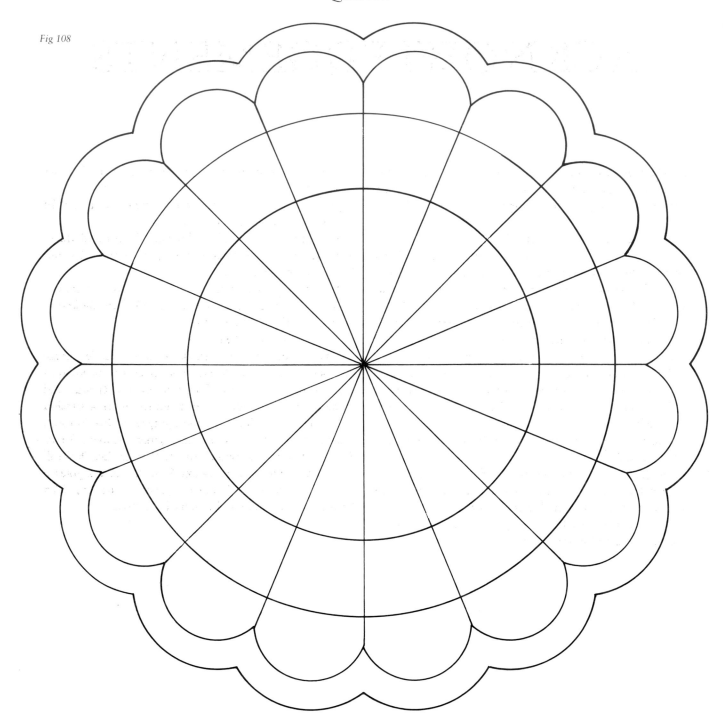

an old blanket, or several layers of blotting paper, or a large corkboard. Put a large sheet of good-quality tracing paper on top and lay the quilt over it. The side of the quilt which shows the quilting lines best should be on top. Prick carefully through every other quilting stitch and eventually you will have a dotted record of the pattern on the tracing paper. Join the dots with a pencil and then go over the lines with a black marker. File patterns with a photo of the quilt and put a clear note of the pattern source on the tracing itself.

QUILTS AS VALUABLES

It is worth insuring any quilts (new or old) in your possession. We can justify insuring old quilts more readily than contemporary ones, but both should be listed on insurance forms. Accidents and thefts do happen – better to be prepared.

138

ACKNOWLEDGEMENTS

Derek, Anna (who thought of the title) and my mother for believing I could write this book and for their unfailing patience, encouragement and support well beyond the call of duty.

Marianne Grime who first asked about quilting.

Chris Franses, Cath Shearing, Paula Hulme, Doris Durrant, Jane Arthur, Sonia Goodwin, Elaine Hammond, Di Huck, Avril Hopcraft, Ann Jermey, Jennie Langmead, Jane Barff, Linda Maltman, Gill Tanner, Gillian Clarke, Jane Walmsley and Margaret Armstrong for their friendship and encouragement over the years.

Pat Cox for a very special quilting friendship.

All my students, past and present, for their unfailing good humour and readiness to learn and experiment.

Shiela Betterton for so readily sharing her considerable knowledge.

Roger Brown and Ken Goodwin for translating ideas into illustrations.

Jen Jones for sharing her wonderful quilt collection.

Jean Eitel, Carter Houck, Sandra Hatch and Louise Townsend for their valuable comments.

Derek, Terry and Sally Gregory and Maureen Shone for proofreading and moral support.

Amy Emms MBE for the inspiration and example of her work.

Jean Dubois for 'White on White' – a pamphlet deserving of wider acknowledgement.

Vivienne Wells for all her editorial guidance and Maggi McCormick for her understanding and practical good-humoured perseverance.

Margaret Wareham for emergency printer services.

Staff of the City Museum & Art Gallery, Stoke-on-Trent, and Ford Green Hall.

Dr Ruth Vincent Kemp.

Having taken a deliberate decision to include a large number of quilts which have not appeared elsewhere, I must also offer sincere thanks to all the friends and students who responded so positively to verbal persuasion in loaning their quilts to be photographed: Chris Franses, Rosemary Wilde, Jane Arthur, Janet Heaney, Karen Shapley, Margaret Philbin, Helyette Newton, Ilse Oldfield, Helen Whittingham, Margaret Salt, Jennie Langmead, Patricia Cox, Sally Redhead, Jacquie Dudley, Jean Croissant and Bryce and Donna Hamilton.

SELECTED BIBLIOGRAPHY

Bain, George *Celtic Art: The Methods of Construction* Constable 1951, 1984

Beamish Museum *North Country Quilts and Coverlets* Beamish Museum 1987

Benjamin, Bonnie *Sashiko: The Quilting of Japan from traditional to today* Needlearts International 1986

Betterton, Shiela *More Quilts and Coverlets* The American Museum in Britain 1988

Betterton, Shiela *Quilts and Coverlets* The American Museum in Britain 1978

Binney Winslow, Gail *Homage to Amanda* R K Press 1984

Cadness, Henry *Decorative Brushwork and Elementary Design* B T Batsford 1909

Colby, Averil *Quilting* B T Batsford (1972), 1978

Cory, Pepper *Quilting Designs from the Amish* C & T Publishing 1985

Cory, Pepper, *Quilting Designs from Antique Quilts* C & T Publishing 1987

Cox, Patricia *Every Stitch Counts* self-published 1981

Day, Lewis F *Ornamental Design* B T Batsford 1888

Dietrich, Mimi *Happy Endings* That Patchwork Place 1988

Donahue, Nancy *Shadow Trapunto* self-published 1983

Dubois, Jean *Patchwork Quilting with Wool* Dover 1978

Dubois, Jean *White on White* La Plata Press 1982

Emms, Amy, MBE *Amy Emms' Story of Durham Quilting* Search Press 1990

Fanning, Robin & Tony *The Complete Book of Machine Quilting* Chilton 1980

Finley, Ruth E *Old Patchwork Quilts & the Women Who Made Them* Charles T Branford 1929, 1983

Fitzrandolph, Mavis *Traditional Quilting* B T Batsford 1954

Fitzrandolph, Mavis & F M Fletcher *Quilting* Dryad Press 1986

Good Housekeeping *Patchwork and Appliqué* Ebury Press 1981

Good Housekeeping *Quilting and Patchwork* Ebury Press 1983

Gutcheon, Beth *The Perfect Patchwork Primer* Penguin 1973

Hake, Elizabeth *English Quilting Old and New* B T Batsford (1937) 1988

Hall, Carrie A & Rose Kretsinger *The Romance of the Patchwork Quilt* Caxton Printers 1936; Dover rev. ed. 1988

Hargrave, Harriet *Heirloom Machine Quilting* C & T Publishing 1990

Hassell, Carla *You Can Be a Super Quilter* Wallace Homestead 1980

Holstein, Jonathan *The Pieced Quilt* Galahad Books

Houck, Carter & Myron Miller *American Quilts and How to Make Them* Charles Scribners 1975

Ickis, Marguerite *The Standard Book of Quiltmaking and Collecting* Dover 1949

Irwin, John Rice *A People and Their Quilts* Schiffer Publishing 1983

James, Michael *The Quiltmaker's Handbook* Prentice Hall 1978

James, Michael *The Second Quiltmaker's Handbook* Prentice Hall 1981

Jenkins, Susan & Linda Seward *Quilts, the American Story* Harper Collins 1991

Jones, Owen *The Grammar of Ornament* Day & Son 1856; Studio Editions 1986

Leone, Diana *Fine Hand Quilting* Leone Publishing Co. 1986

Leland, Charles G *The Minor Arts & Industries* Whittaker & Co 1893

Lipsett, Linda Otto *Remember Me: Women and their Friendship Quilts* Quilt Digest Press 1985

McClun, Diana & Laura Nownes *Quilts! Quilts! Quilts!* Quilt Digest Press 1988

McClun, Diana & Laura Nownes *Quilts Galore* Quilt Digest Press 1990

Morgan, Mary & Dee Mosteller *Trapunto and Other Forms of Raised Quilting* Charles Scribner 1977

Morris, Pat *The Ins and Outs: Perfecting the Quilting Stitch* American Quilters Society 1990

Osler, Dorothy *Quilting* Merehurst 1991

Osler, Dorothy *Traditional British Quilts* B T Batsford 1987

Ota, Kimi *Sashiko Quilting* self-published 1981

Petrie, Flinders *Decorative Patterns of the Ancient World* Studio Editions (1930) 1990

Pottinger, David *Quilts from the Indiana Amish* E.P. Dutton 1983

Rae, Janet *Quilts of the British Isles* Constable 1987

Rodgers, Sue *Trapunto: the Book of Stuffed Quilting* Moon Over the Mountain Publishing Co. 1990

Seward, Linda *The Complete Book of Patchwork, Quilting and Appliqué* Mitchell Beazley 1987

Simms, Ami *How to Improve Your Quilting Stitch* self-published 1986

Squire, Helen *Dear Helen, Can You Tell Me* American Quilters Society 1987

Thompson, Shirley *The Finishing Touch* Powell Publications 1980

Thompson, Shirley *It's Not a Quilt Until It's Quilted* Powell Publications 1984

Walker, Michelle *Quiltmaking in Patchwork* Ebury Press 1985

Walker, Michelle *The Passionate Quilter* Ebury Press 1990

Webster, Marie D *Quilts: Their Story and How to Make Them* Doubleday 1915 (reprinted as Practical Patchwork 1990)

USEFUL ADDRESSES

The following list of quilt shops, suppliers, periodicals, guilds, societies, shows and museums is not intended to be in any way comprehensive. It is always advisable to check before planning any visit.

QUILT SHOPS

UNITED KINGDOM

Village Fabrics
Lester Way
Wallingford, Oxfordshire OX10 9DD

The Country Store
68 Westbourne Road
Marsh
Huddersfield, W Yorks

Strawberry Fayre
Chagford
Newton Abbot, Devon TQ13 8EN

The Quilt Room
20 West Street
Dorking, Surrey RH4 1BL

Pansy Pins
159 Main Street
Uddingston
Glasgow G71 7BP

Many other quilt shops can be found in the advertisement sections of needlework and quilting magazines.

UNITED STATES

An invaluable guide to the quilting 'scene' in the United States is the *Quilters Sourcebook*, Anne Patterson Dee, Wallace Homestead (1987).

Quilts and other Comforts
P.O. Box 394–226
Wheatridge, CO 80034–0394

Gutcheon Patchworks
11002 Valley Avenue East
Puyallup, WA 98372

Great Expectations
14520 Memorial Drive #54
Houston, TX 77089

Glad Creations
3400 Bloomington Ave. So.
Minneapolis, MN 55407

Empty Spools
70 Bradley
Walnut Creek, CA 94596

Strawberry Patch
Columbia Crossroads, PA 16914

Hancock Fabrics
3841 Hinterville Road, Interstate #24
Paducah, KY 42001

A huge number of quilt shops exists, many of which advertise in quilting magazines.

AUSTRALIA

The Calico Patch
O'Hanlon Place
Gungahlin, ACT 2912

Truly Lois
4 Victoria Street
Hall, ACT 2618

Anne's Glory Box
60–62 Beaumont Street
Hamilton, NSW 2303

Berrima Patchwork & Craft
Hume Highway
Berrima, NSW 2577

The Lighthouse Cottage Quilters
122 Princes Highway
Milton, NSW 2538

Patches 'N' Pieces
32 Oxford Street
Epping, NSW 2121

The Quilting Bee
Shop 14, Gordon Village Arcade
Gordon, NSW 2072

Rose Brier Patchwork Shop
Shop 6, Penrith Centre Shopping Mall
Penrith, NSW 2750

Tricia's Gather 'N' Stitch
1 Faucett Street
Blackalls Park, NSW 2282

Alice Traders
2 Schwartz Crescent
Alice Springs, NT 0870

Krafty Kats
Shop 14, Robina Shopping Village
Robina, QLD 4226

Patches Indooroopilly
9 Railway Avenue
Indooroopilly, QLD 4068

Patchwork Supplies
43 Gloucester Street
Highgate Hill, QLD 4101

Patchwork Tree
43 Denman Street
Alderley, QLD 4051

Quilters Store
1 Manning Street
Milton, QLD 4064

Country Patch Works
34 James Street
Mount Gambier, SA 5290

Barossa Quilt & Craft Cottage
Angaston Road
Nurioopta, SA 5355

Patches & Pieces
14 Belvidere Road
Saddleworth, SA 5413

The Quilt Basket
102 Main Street
Yankalilla, SA 5203

Quilters Cupboard
Shop 11, Village Market Place
Hahndorf, SA 5245

Quilts & Threads
Shop 3, 1015 Lower North East Road
Highbury, SA 5089

American Patchworks
91 Patrick Street
Hobart, TAS 7000

Knit 'N' Sew
49 King Street
Scottsdale, TAS 7260

Patchwork House
77 Church Street
Hawthorn, VIC 3122

Patchwork Plus
464 High Street
East Kew, VIC 3102

Threadbare Quilters
56 Hargraves Street
Castlemaine, VIC 3450

Calico House
2 Napoleon Street
Cottesloe, WA 6011

Country Patchwork Cottage
10/86 Erindale Road
Balcatta, WA 6021

Patchworks of WA
394 Fitzgerald Street
North Perth, WA 6006

NEW ZEALAND

Canvas Craft
PO Box 825
Blenheim

Jan's Patch
235 Moray Place
Dunedin

Karori Wool & Patchwork
148 Karori Road
Wellington

Patchwork Barn
132 Hinemoa Street
Birkenhead
Auckland

Sewing Box
Courtville Place
101 Dee Street
Invercargill

Wool & Handcraft Shop
221 Heretaunga Street East
Hastings

QUILTING MAGAZINES/ PERIODICALS

Patchwork and Quilting
1 Highfield Close
Malvern Link, Worcs, UK

Quilters Newsletter
Leman Publications
6700 West 44 Avenue
Wheatridge, CO 80033, USA

Ladies Circle Patchwork Quilts
Lopez Publications
105 East 35 Street
New York, NY 10016, USA

Quilt
Harris Publications
1115 Broadway
New York, NY 10010, USA

Traditional Quiltworks and **Quilting Today**
Chitra Publications
301 Church Street
PO Box 437
New Milford, PA 18834–0437, USA

Down Under Quilts
PO Box 619
Beenleigh, QLD 4207, Australia

New Zealand Quilter
PO Box 9202
Wellington, New Zealand

GUILDS AND ORGANISATIONS

UNITED KINGDOM

Quilters Guild
OP 66
Dean Clough
Halifax HX3 5AX

National Patchwork Association
PO Box 300
Hethersett
Norwich NR9 3DB

UNITED STATES

National Quilting Association
PO Box 393
Ellicott City, MD 21043–0393

American Quilters Society
PO Box 3290
Paducah, KY 42002–3290

AUSTRALIA

Australian Quilters
PO Box 479
Armidale, NSW 2350

Australian Quilters Association
PO Box 497
Hawthorn, VIC 3122

Canberra Quilters Inc
PO Box 29
Jamison Centre, ACT 2614

Darwin Patchworkers & Quilters Inc
PO Box 36945
Winnellie, NT 0821

Patchworkers & Quilters Guild of Victoria Inc
Secretary
8 Belinda Avenue
Research, VIC 3095

Queensland Quilters Inc
GPO Box 2841
Brisbane, QLD 4001

Quilters' Guild Inc
PO Box 654
Neutral Bay Junction, NSW 2089

Quilters Guild of South Australia Inc
PO Box 993
Norwood, SA 5067

West Australian Quilters Association
PO Box 188
Subiaco, WA 6008

NEW ZEALAND

Quilt Symposium '93
PO Box 11 051
Wellington

Many groups and organisations exist worldwide. If you are not aware of any nearby, ask at the local library and check the classified sections of the magazines listed opposite.

ANNUAL QUILT SHOWS

UNITED KINGDOM

Quilts UK (May)
1 Highfield Close
Malvern Link, Worcs WR14 1SH

Great British Quilt Festival (August)
13 Stourton Road
Ainsdale
Southport, Merseyside PR8 2PL

National Patchwork Championships (June)
PO Box 300
Hethersett, Norwich NR9 3DB

UNITED STATES

Houston International Quilt Festival (November)
14520 Memorial #54
Houston, TX 77079

Quilt shows of every size abound in the United States; check the classified section of quilting magazines for up-to-date details.

MUSEUMS

Many museums have quilts in their collections which may not be on permanent view. A list of museums to visit in the UK is available from The Quilters Guild.

It is always advisable to check opening times before travelling!

The American Museum in Britain
Claverton Manor
Bath, Avon BA2 7BD, UK

Beamish Open Air Museum
Beamish
Stanley, Co. Durham DH9 0RG, UK

Welsh Folk Museum
St Fagans
Cardiff CF5 6XB, UK

Ulster Folk and Transport Museum
Cultra Manor
Holywood, Co. Down BT18 0EU, UK

The Metropolitan Museum of Art
5th Avenue at 82nd Street
New York, NY 10028, USA

Daughters of the American Revolution Museum
1776 Main Street
Washington, DC, USA

Shelburne Museum
Shelburne, VT, USA

Smithsonian Institution
20560 Constitution Avenue
Washington, DC 20560, USA

Cooper-Hewitt Museum
2 East 91st Street
New York, NY 10028, USA

INDEX